BICYCLE
REPAIR
MANUAL

BICYCLE REPAIR MANUAL

CHRIS SIDWELLS

SIXTH EDITION
Senior Editor Richard Gilbert
Editor Kate Taylor
Senior Art Editor Helen Spencer
Managing Editor Gareth Jones
Managing Art Editor Lee Griffiths
Pre-Production Jacqueline Street
Producer Mandy Inness
Jacket Designer Surabhi Wadhwa
Jacket Editor Claire Gell
Jacket Design Development Manager
Sophia MTT

FIRST EDITION
Editor Pip Morgan
Designers Edward Kinsey, Peter Laws
Technical Consultant Guy Andrews

This American Edition, 2017
First American Edition, 2004
Published in the United States by DK Publishing
345 Hudson Street, New York, New York 10014

Contents

Introduction

A clean, well-maintained bike will work efficiently and safely, and add to your enjoyment of cycling by giving you peace of mind.

Safety and efficiency are closely linked. If your gears are not shifting correctly, for instance, they will not only affect your riding efficiency, but also tempt you to look down at them while riding to see what is causing the problem. As a result, you might take your eyes off what is happening on the road ahead and expose yourself to the possibility of a collision. The *Bicycle Repair Manual* will help you avoid such problems by demonstrating how to maintain your bike regularly and correctly.

Understanding technology

Modern bikes may seem complicated, and the technology that manufacturers use may be more sophisticated than ever. However, cycle components work, as they always have, according to logical principles, so there is no reason for you to be daunted.

Before you begin to service a particular component of your bike, first become familiar with the part by turning to the relevant section. Knowing how a part works makes it easier to maintain.

Above all, be confident and patient with what you are doing. Even if you do not think of yourself as mechanically minded, you may come to enjoy bike maintenance after a while and you will certainly enjoy the trouble-free cycling that rewards your efforts.

Collecting information

If you buy a new bike, make sure that you keep the accompanying owner's manual, so that you can refer to it alongside this book. Do the same with any new equipment that you buy.

If your bike is not new, obtain a manual from a bike shop or the manufacturer's website. Manuals will help you be aware of the particular maintenance requirements of all the components of your bike.

If you want to learn more about bike mechanics, there are many magazines available that contain tips on specific components. However, the large majority of people who are simply interested in learning how to maintain their bike will find everything they need to know in the pages of the *Bicycle Repair Manual*.

Using this book

The different maintenance requirements of the most common types of bikes are listed at the beginning of the book. These requirements are covered in the step-by-step pages that are specific to the components installed on each type of bike—for example, suspension forks on mountain bikes.

You will also find a timetable for servicing the parts of your bike and a troubleshooting chart to help you identify and solve problems. The book helps you spot danger signs and carry out routine safety checks. These features detail what you need to do and refer you to the relevant step-by-step sequences that explain how to do it.

GETTING TO KNOW YOUR BIKE

Understanding your bike will make it easier to maintain. Identify all the different parts and components to help you see how they work together as a whole.

The basic bike

Modern bikes, such as the hybrid bike (*below*), are designed to be light and user-friendly. Each part performs a key function in the overall operation of the bike.

The frame is the skeleton to which all components are attached. The fork holds the front wheel, and connects to the handlebars so the bike can be steered. Suspension forks improve comfort and control over rough surfaces. The drivetrain is the system that transfers the rider's energy, via the pedals and cranks, to the rear wheel. It also contains a number of sprockets, known as chainrings and cogs, which carry the chain.

The derailleurs change the bike's gears by moving the chain onto different chainrings and cogs. Derailleurs are controlled by the gear-shift levers, which are mounted on the handlebar to allow quick and easy use by the rider. The brakes are controlled by

Hybrid bike ▶
Advances in technology have refined the design and improved the performance of each category of bike part, producing a machine that is easy to ride and maintain.

Wheel (*see pp.114–15, 118–23*)
The rim's shape and high-tech aluminum increase the wheel's strength. Wheels with disc brakes, shown here, can have lighter rims than bikes with rim brakes.

Derailleur (*see pp.64–9*)
Derailleurs are designed to cope with the wide range of sprocket sizes required to climb and descend the steepest hills.

Frame (*see pp.12–13*)
Improved welding techniques allow thin-walled aluminum tubes to provide a relatively cheap, light, and responsive frame. The thickness of the tube walls varies to cope with areas of increased stress.

Pedal (*see pp.92–99*)
Clipless pedals allow more power to be transferred to the wheels because the feet are fixed to the pedals. Flat pedals, and toe clips and straps, are simpler and easier to use.

Drivetrain (*see pp.70–91*)
Stiff materials maximize the amount of power the drivetrain transfers to the rear wheel. A triple crankset increases gear range and a flexible chain allows quick, easy gear-shifts.

brake levers that are also mounted on the handlebar, and use brake pads to press against the wheel's rim, or discs attached to the hub, to stop the bike.

High-tech machine ▶
Many years of design refinement have produced an adaptable hybrid bike, which combines technology from road and mountain bikes for use in an urban environment.

Gear-shift levers
(*see pp.52–9*)
Ergonomically designed gear-shift levers were developed from mountain bikes, and give easy, precise gear-shifts.

Fork (*see pp.150–61*)
Forks are designed with varying thickness in the tube wall. Tubes are thin in the middle and thick at both ends. This reduces weight and absorbs road shock. Some forks also act as suspension systems, further reducing shock and improving control.

Brake (*see pp.124–47*)
Disc brakes offer sensitive, powerful braking that is not affected by weather conditions. Other bikes have rim brakes, which are still very good, although they require earlier braking to slow in wet weather.

Tire (*see pp.120–21*)
Modern tires are made from rubber compounds that roll well on the road, while adhering to it when cornering. They often have puncture-resistant bands of material, such as Kevlar, beneath the tread.

Anatomy of the bike

Understanding how the parts on your bike fit together will help you perform maintenance tasks successfully. Although your bike may differ from the modern mountain bike (*right*), all bikes fit together in a similar way. For example, the quick-release levers on the wheels below perform the same function as axle nuts on a bike with hub gears.

The main parts and their components, and where each part is attached to the bike, are shown on the mountain bike. Take the time to study the illustration, since it will act as a useful reference to help you follow the steps later in the book.

Mountain bike ▶
The mountain bike is a good example of how parts fit together—its frame, wheels, drivetrain, pedals, derailleurs, brakes, and gear-shift levers are similar to those of road and hybrid bikes.

Saddle
Saddle cover
Saddle rails

Seat post
Saddle clamp

Rear brake
Cable-guide tube
Braking surface
Brake pad
Brake arm

Frame
Seat tube
Seat stay
Chainstay
Down tube

Rear hub
Rear drop-out
Hub
Quick-release

Bottom bracket

Cassette
Cassette body
Cog
Lockring

Rear derailleur
Jockey pulley
Derailleur plate
Barrel adjuster

Bike controls

Gear-shift lever

Handlebar

Grip

Brake lever

THE ASSEMBLED BIKE

Bike parts are designed to bolt together in the same way to allow straightforward maintenance by following a few key workshop principles (*see pp.34–5*). Most parts use Allen bolts, so for many tasks an Allen key multi-tool is all that is required.

Steering

Handlebar stem

Top cup and bearing

Spacer

Stem cap

Head tube

Top tube

Steerer tube

Bottom cup and bearing

Front wheel

Hub

Spoke

Rim

Fork crown

Fork blade

Slider

Quick-release

Tires

Tire bead

Valve

Tire

Inner tube

Drivetrain

Right-hand crankarm

Chainring

Front derailleur

Chain

Pedal

Pedal body

Foot retention mechanism

Pedal axle

Bikes for general use

You can buy a bike for almost any purpose, but even a simple utility, hybrid, or folding bike will increase your fitness, save you money on train or bus tickets, and have no negative impact on your environment.

As long as the bike is of good quality, you will only need to keep it clean and check it regularly for signs of wear. Hybrid bikes, utility bikes, and folding bikes are all dependable machines that are suitable for commuting to work or school, day-to-day transportation, or simply a relaxing ride on a bike trail or country road.

The hybrid bike
Lightweight materials combined with road bike performance and hardy mountain bike technology make hybrid bikes perfect for bumpy urban roads. They are ideal for commuting, family rides, fitness riding, touring, and carrying luggage.

The utility bike
Utility bikes are ideal for local commuting and short rides. They are equipped with fat tires that absorb road bumps but will drag on long journeys, making them tiring and uncomfortable to ride.

The folding bike
Ideal for commuters, and for people with little space in which to store a standard bike, folding bikes can go anywhere, especially on public transportation. The folded bike can be easily reassembled into a serviceable machine without the use of tools.

Urban commuting
With its head-up, traffic-friendly riding position and easy-to-operate gears, the lightweight hybrid is ideal for urban commuting.

ESSENTIAL MAINTENANCE CHECKLIST

HYBRID BIKE

- Regularly maintain and lubricate the derailleur gears (see pp.66–9).
- Check the gear cables for signs of wear (see p.47, pp.58–9).
- Check the brake cables or hoses, and pads for signs of wear (see p.47, pp.130–1).
- Check the tires for signs of wear (see p.47).
- Regularly change the chain (see pp.76–7).

Tire

Rear derailleur

Front derailleur

Chain

Gear cable

Brake cable

UTILITY BIKE

- Regularly lubricate the hub gears (see pp.72–3).
- Regularly check the gear cables for signs of wear (see p.47).
- Regularly check the brake control cables for signs of wear (see pp.130–1).
- Regularly check the brake pads for signs of wear (see p.46).
- Regularly clean and grease the chain (see pp.36–9).

Sprung saddle

Brake lever

Hub gears

Handlebar basket

Chainguard

FOLDING BIKE

- Regularly check and lubricate the pivots and the locks that allow the bike to fold and unfold.
- Regularly check hub gears, even though they are shielded from the elements and thus need very little maintenance (see pp.72–3).
- Pay extra attention to the outer control cables (see p.47, pp.58–9).

Rear suspension

Hub and derailleur gear system

Folded bike

Frame hinge

Large chainrings

Unfolded bike

Specialized bikes

If you want to take up cycling as a hobby, rather than as a means of transportation, look for a more specialized bike, such as a road bike, a mountain bike, or a triathlon bike.

As bikes become more sophisticated they need more care. For example, lightweight parts wear out quickly, so they must be kept scrupulously clean. Hydraulic disc brakes and suspension systems need regular attention. Electronic gear systems need their batteries recharged. Paintwork and lightweight frames (especially carbon fiber) can be damaged by flying stones. Have any major dent, and certainly any crack, checked by a professional.

Do not let this deter you from buying your dream bike. Just as riding it will be a joy, maintaining it to exacting standards will be part of the whole cycling experience.

The road bike

Lightweight materials and narrow tires make road bikes good for fitness riding, day touring, and competitions. The aerodynamic position afforded by a drop handlebar offers great speed. Road bikes are so light and have such a range of gears that almost anyone, with a little training, can tackle the great mountain passes made famous by the Tour de France.

The mountain bike

Full-suspension mountain bikes allow you to break new ground and ride across rugged terrain that was previously unthinkable and at speeds that were once unattainable.

The triathlon and time-trial bike

This type of bike is used in triathlons and time-trial races, where competitors cannot draft behind each other, so the bike must be as aerodynamic as possible. The bike's geometry allows the rider to get low and narrow, smoothing the air flow over them.

Road riding
This road bike represents the ultimate in road bike design, and is the type of bike that professionals use in the Tour de France.

ESSENTIAL MAINTENANCE CHECKLIST

ROAD BIKE

- Regularly clean and lubricate the bike (see pp.36–9).
- Make routine safety checks (see pp.40–1).
- Check the brakes (see pp.132–3).
- Make sure the gears are working perfectly (see pp.66–9).
- Check frame protector pads for wear in the locations where cable outers touch carbon-fiber frames (see p.41).

Carbon-fiber frame

Aluminum drop handlebar

Caliper brake

Electronic gear-shift system

Road race tire

Clipless pedal

Lightweight wheels

MOUNTAIN BIKE

- Set up the suspension fork and rear shock (see pp.152–9, 164–5).
- Regularly clean and lubricate the suspension (see pp.160–1).
- Regularly inspect pivots (see pp.166–7) and seals.
- Check brake cables or hoses, and pads (see pp.46–7, 130–1, 140–1).
- Replace the cassette every six months (see pp.80–1).
- Service the headset regularly (see pp.104–7).

Carbon-fiber frame

Straight handlebar

Rear shock

Wheels come in 26-, 27.5-, and 29-inch sizes

Rear derailleur

Suspension fork

Disc brake

TRIATHLON AND TIME-TRIAL BIKE

- Regularly inspect the frame and any carbon-fiber wheels for signs of cracks (see pp.40–1).
- Tires on tri-bikes are light and thin—check them for cuts, splits, and bulges (see p.47).
- Make sure the gears are shifting perfectly, and replace cables if necessary (see pp.56–7).
- Maintain and adjust brakes so they can be applied with minimum force (see pp.132–3).

Integrated aero bars for a low, narrow riding position

Electronic bar-end shifters

Aerodynamic frame

Carbon-fiber disc wheel

Deep section carbon-fiber front wheel

Deep chainrings improve air flow

Bikes for enthusiasts

Many cyclists become enthusiasts for particular kinds of bikes. These bikes might not be designed for different terrains or for competing—rather they might be designs that suit a lifestyle or are fun to ride.

These examples all require general and some specific maintenance, although a big appeal of BMX and fixed-gear bikes is their simplicity of design, making them easy to maintain. Tandems have maintenance needs due to the double load they carry.

The fixed-gear bike

One of the simplest bikes, these have a single "fixed" gear, meaning that the pedals must turn constantly for the wheel to rotate. They are perfect for everyday use and are simple to maintain. Some have a "flip-flop" hub, which also contains a freewheel.

The BMX

BMXs are made for acceleration and agile bike handling. Like some of the very first bicycles, they are made almost entirely from steel because it transfers power in a way that no other material can.

The tandem

A bicycle made for two must be twice as strong, but it is also twice as hard to stop. Brake maintenance is crucial. So is having a well-maintained, smooth-shifting drivetrain.

Riding fixed
Fixed-gear bikes are ideal for year-round use—their lack of gears means they can function in all weather with little maintenance.

ESSENTIAL MAINTENANCE CHECKLIST

BMX

- Regularly check the bottom bracket to make sure it is running free, but not loose.
- Replace the pedals if their axles are bent (see pp.94–5).
- Adjust the brakes to ensure a minimum of travel before the brakes come on, as the steel rims, although very strong, do not make good braking surfaces.

Single gearing

Gyro headset

Stunt peg

Opposite transmission

FIXED-GEAR

- Regularly inspect the bottom bracket, steering, and wheel bearings to make sure they are running free but have no play (see pp.86–9, 104–7, 116–17).
- Make sure the wheel nuts are tight before each ride (see pp.78–9).
- Check brakes for excessive travel (see pp.132–7).
- Check pedals for damage and wear (see pp.94–5).

Single gear, sometimes with flip-flop hub

Straight handlebar

Large-flange hubs

Deep-section rims

Hard-wearing clipless pedals

TANDEM

- Check brakes for excessive travel and pad wear (see pp.132–7, 140–3).
- Check the chain for wear, and clean and lubricate it regularly (see pp.36–9, 76–7).
- Check the wheels for trueness and wear—tandem wheels are put under great stress (see pp.122–3).
- Check the longer cable lengths for wear (see p.47).

Pilot's saddle

Pilot's handlebar

Robust frame with extra-thick tubes

Stoker's handlebar

Cantilever brakes

Stoker's saddle

Crossover drivetrain

Two pairs of pedals

Setting up an adult's bike

If the saddle's height and angle are adjusted and the position of the brake levers on the handlebar is set so that they are within easy reach, then riding will be more efficient and comfortable. A novice cyclist should try setting the saddle height a little lower at first, and work toward the ideal once he or she is used to riding.

STEP LOCATOR

Toolbox
- Allen key multi-tool ● Wrenches
- Screwdriver

Adjusting your riding position

1 **Remove your shoes** and sit on your bike, supporting yourself against a wall.

● Set your crankarms so that the pedal farthest from the wall is at the low point of its revolution.

● Put the heel of your foot on the pedal. Your leg should be straight when you do this. Ask someone to help you check.

The knee aligns with the axle

4 **Place the widest part** of your foot over the pedal axle. If your shoes have cleats, set them up so that your foot can easily adopt this position (see pp.98–9).

● Set your crankarms parallel to the floor. The depression on the side of your leading leg, just behind the kneecap, should be directly over the axle of the pedal. Ask your helper to check.

5 **Move your saddle back** if the depression on your leg is in front of the axle. If it is behind, move it forward.

● Undo the saddle clamp under the saddle. On modern bikes, you will need an Allen key; on older bikes, use a wrench.

● Repeat Steps 4 and 5 until you are sure you have the position right.

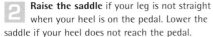

2 **Raise the saddle** if your leg is not straight when your heel is on the pedal. Lower the saddle if your heel does not reach the pedal.

● Undo the seat pin clamp bolt. Raise or lower the saddle, tighten up the bolt, and try again. Ask your helper to see if your leg is straight. Do not lean on the foot that you are testing.

3 **To make absolutely sure** the saddle height is right for you, go for a ride with your cycling shoes on and your feet in their normal position on the pedals.

● Ask your helper to ride behind you and make sure that your hips are not rocking from side to side as you ride. If they are, the saddle is set too high and you need to repeat Steps 1 and 2.

6 **Make sure that the brake reach** allows you to apply the brakes using the first joints of your first two fingers, while holding the handlebar securely with your thumb and remaining fingers. You should be able to hook your fingers over the brake levers. If you have to stretch too far, you will be unable to apply enough power.

7 **Adjust the reach** of the brake levers if you have to stretch too far.

● Undo the brake cable (see pp.134–5) and screw in the adjuster on the lever until you can reach it easily. Then reclamp the brake cables.

● Set the brake levers at an angle to the handlebar so that you can pull them in line with your arm.

Setting up a road bike

When setting up your road bike, the aerodynamics of your position are especially important, since road bikes are designed for speed. Your aim is to be efficient so that your pedaling energy is turned into forward motion, and you sit in a way that doesn't impede your progress by increasing drag. You also need to be comfortable and in control.

STEP LOCATOR

Toolbox

• Allen key multi-tool • Straight edge

Adjusting your riding position

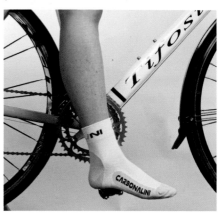

1 **Remove your cycling shoes** and get on your bike, supporting yourself on a wall or with the rear wheel mounted on a turbo trainer.

• Set your cranks so that the pedal farthest from the wall is at the low point of its revolution.

• Sit level in the saddle, not favoring either side, and place your heel on the pedal. Your saddle is at the correct height when your leg is straight.

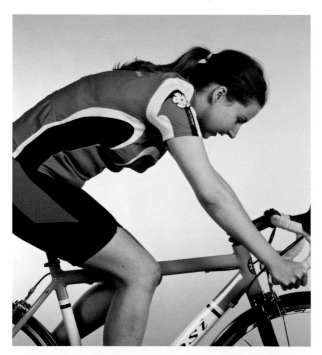

4 **To check your stem length,** sit on your bike with your feet on the pedals, holding the bottom of the bar.

• Look down at the front-wheel hub. It should be obscured by the handlebar. If the hub is in front of the bar, your stem is too short; if it is behind the bar, your stem is too long.

• If you have to change your stem, measure it and figure out how much longer or shorter the new stem needs to be. Remove and replace it (see pp.104–5).

• Back-pedal, sitting in the same position. If your upper leg touches your stomach and feels like it will restrict breathing, raise your handlebar. To do this, swap the headset spacers (see pp.104–5) or install a shallower handlebar (see pp.110–11).

Knee aligns with pedal axle

2 **Lower your saddle** if your heel doesn't touch the pedal. Raise it if your heel touches the pedal but your leg is bent.

● Undo the seat bolt—an Allen bolt on most road bikes—adjust the saddle height, and retighten it.

● While pedaling, ask someone to stand behind you and make sure your hips don't rock up and down with each revolution—a sign that the saddle is too high. Lower the saddle if this occurs.

3 **To set the optimum** fore-and-aft position of your saddle on the seat post, place the widest part of your foot over the pedal axle.

● With your cranks horizontal, the depression on the outside of your knee—just behind the knee cap—should be directly over the pedal axle.

● To achieve this, undo the saddle-clamp bolt under your saddle and shift it forward or back on the seat post, then retighten the bolt.

5 **The optimum position for brake levers** is for the tip of each lever to line up with the flat section at the bottom of the handlebar.

● Place a straight edge against the underside of the flat section. Peel back the brake-lever cover to expose the clamp bolt. Loosen it with an Allen key.

● Move the lever up or down to align the lever tip with the straight edge. You may have to remove the handlebar tape to achieve this (see pp.110–11).

6 **Adjust the handlebar angle** until it feels comfortable to ride with your hands on the brake levers, and to apply the brakes while holding the lower section of the handlebar.

● Loosen the stem's handlebar-clamp bolts and twist the handlebar to angle it up or down. The optimum position for you can only be found by trying several different positions, but extreme handlebar angles should be avoided.

Setting up a child's bike

Before a child starts riding a bike, adjust the saddle and handlebar to suit his or her body. Set the saddle at its lowest point, as in Step 1. Buy the biggest bike possible at first, then keep adjusting it as the child grows taller. Children's bikes are usually measured by wheel size—from 12in (30cm) up to 24in (60cm).

STEP LOCATOR

Toolbox

- Allen key multi-tool ● Wrenches
- Plastic mallet

Adjusting the position of the saddle

1 **Set the saddle** on your child's bike at a height that allows him or her to sit on it and simultaneously touch the ground with the front part of each foot. This is the ideal setup.

Adjusting the height of the handlebar

1 **Raise or lower the bike's handlebar** by loosening the expander bolt that holds the stem in the bike. This bolt is secured by either an Allen bolt or a hexagonal bolt, so use an Allen key or a wrench to loosen it.

- Knock the bolt down with a plastic mallet to free it up if you need to.

2 **Grip the front wheel** between your legs to steady it and then pull the handlebar up or push it down. Do not pull the handlebar higher than the safety limit that is marked on the stem. Once the handlebar is at the right height, and the stem is lined up with the front wheel, tighten the expander bolt.

2 **Loosen the seat pin clamp**—it has either a quick-release lever or a nut-and-bolt fixing that requires a wrench. Either pull the saddle up or push it down to the required height.

3 **Move the saddle** forward or backward by loosening the nut that secures the seat clamp. Tighten the nut again, but be sure that the saddle is parallel to the ground.

3 **Adjust the saddle** and handlebar still further if you need to, so that your child can sit in the ideal riding position— neither too upright, nor too stretched.

Accessorizing your bike

There are a number of accessories that can be attached to your bike. If you ride during the hours of darkness, you have a legal duty to display a white light at the front and a red light at the rear of your bike.

A range of lights is available to fit any bike, but some accessories, such as bottle cages and child seats, require there to be threaded fixing bosses on the bike's frame. Also, any child carried in a child seat must wear a bike helmet specifically designed for their age.

Other useful accessories include bike locks, which are essential if you leave your bike in a public place, and saddle bags, which are the best place to store spares, such as a spare inner tube, tire levers, and a multi-tool.

Child seat

Rear light

Front light

U-lock

Bottle cage

Affixing accessories
Position items so that they do not interfere with one another. The child seat obscures the rear light, so it would have to be removed at night.

Lights

There are various attachment methods for lights, but the most popular types clip onto a bracket bolted to the handlebar (front lights) or seat post (rear lights). This means the lights can be easily unclipped so you can take them with you when you leave your bike.

Bottle cage

Cages can be mounted on your bike that are made specifically to carry drink bottles. This allows you to take a drink on your rides, which helps prevent possible dehydration. There are usually two sets of bosses on bike frames—one set on the downtube and one set on the seat tube.

Lock

Bike locks, like this U-lock, are essential for securing your bike in public areas. They can be carried on a mount—usually supplied with the lock when you buy it—that fits onto your bike frame. Follow the manufacturer's installation instructions and check periodically to make sure the mount is secure. Check for cracks on it too.

Saddle bag

Bags fit under the saddle by means of velcro loops or a mount that is fixed to the saddle rails, as is the case with this one. The bag can then be clipped on and off the mount, or the velcro released. Most bags come with instructions and they must be followed exactly, for ease of use and for safety reasons. Make sure your bag is securely mounted before each ride.

Child seat

1 **Every child seat** has a mount that attaches to your bike, and the seat is then attached to the mount.

● This mount is a pannier rack, which fits a bike that has threaded pannier bosses on its frame. Assemble the mount, then apply grease to the bolts that attach it to the frame.

● Screw the mounting bolts into the pannier bosses, fixing the rack to the frame.

2 **With the rack** securely mounted on your bike, you can attach the seat to it.

● Again, there will be specific instructions supplied with each make and type of seat. Follow them carefully, ensuring that the bolts are tight.

● Fit the child's safety harness, plus the padding and grips provided by the manufacturer for comfort and safety.

3 **Some seats have** an extra fail-safe device. This seat has a safety strap that anchors the seat to the bike's seat post.

● It's a good idea to inspect the seat and its mount, checking every bolt for tightness, after the first ride with a child sitting in it.

● Check the seat and its mount periodically, depending on how often you use it.

Installing a cyclocomputer and GPS

Feedback is a great spur to riding, which is why cyclocomputers are useful. Knowing how fast and how far you have traveled, and even how much altitude you have gained, adds another dimension to your riding.

It's also good to know where you're going. It encourages you to try new routes and explore. GPS devices do just that, as well as many of the things that cyclocomputers do.

STEP LOCATOR

Parts of a cyclocomputer and GPS unit

Cyclocomputer and parts

Sensor

Computer

Magnet

Cadence sensor

GPS unit and parts

GPS unit

Crank magnet

Toolbox

- Small screwdriver or Allen keys (as necessary)
- Cable cutters or scissors (to trim cable ties)

Installing a cyclocomputer

1 **Install the magnet** to a spoke on one of your bike's wheels. The manufacturer's instructions will say which wheel and exactly how to attach it. Magnets come in two varieties: either in two halves that fit around a spoke, or as a unit that clips onto a spoke.

- This magnet fits around a spoke. Open it up (*inset*), put one half on one side of your chosen spoke, then attach the other half to hold it in place.

3 **Attach the computer mount** to your handlebar. This mount is secured with cable ties, but others may be affixed with a clamp and bolt. Make sure the mount fits securely.

- This is a wireless model, but if yours has a wire connecting the sensor and mount, attach it to your fork with cable ties, then wind it around the front-brake cable-outer until level with the handlebar. Allow enough slack so as not to impede steering.

Installing a GPS unit

2 Attach the sensor to your bike. This one is attached to the fork with cable ties. Follow the instructions, and make sure that the correct side of the sensor is facing the spokes.

● Line the sensor up with the magnet. There is often a light indicator on the sensor to show that it has detected the magnet. Turn the wheel to run the magnet past the sensor a few times, then adjust the sensor until the light flashes.

1 Attach any ancillary devices first. This GPS unit has a pedal-cadence sensor, which requires a magnet to be fitted to the left-hand crank. Then the sensor is attached to the left-hand chainstay with cable ties.

● Make sure the sensor and magnet of any ancillary devices line up before continuing.

4 Program your computer by following the manufacturer's instructions, then clip it to the handlebar mount.

● If the computer has a heart-rate function, it's worth making sure that it works while you are seated on the bike. If it doesn't work, you might have to mount the computer on your bike's stem to bring it within range of the sensor, which you wear on a chest strap.

2 Attach the GPS mount to the handlebars or the stem.

● Some mounts are attached with bolted clamps, but this one is secured with an elastic loop.

● Program the GPS unit, following the instructions that came with it, or the prompts that appear on the screen when switched on. Then clip the unit onto the mount (*inset*).

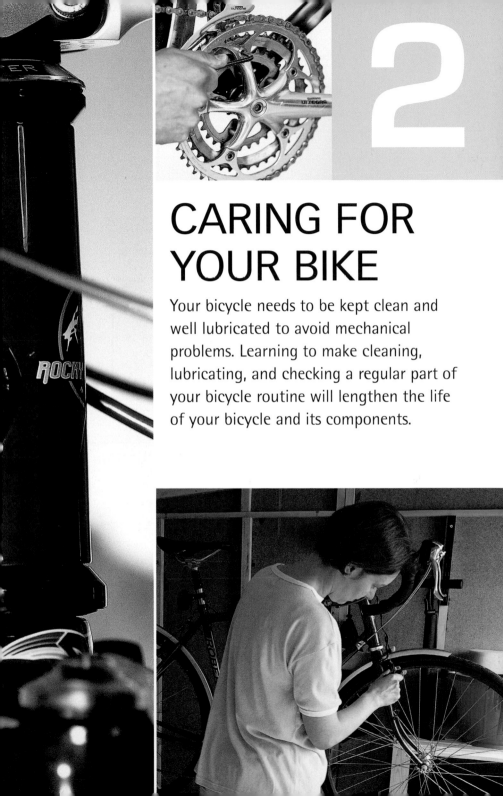

CARING FOR YOUR BIKE

Your bicycle needs to be kept clean and well lubricated to avoid mechanical problems. Learning to make cleaning, lubricating, and checking a regular part of your bicycle routine will lengthen the life of your bicycle and its components.

Tools

If you are going to regularly maintain and repair your bike, you will need to buy a tool kit or assemble your own. The tools shown opposite will enable you to carry out all the essential repairs and maintain your bike at peak performance. Add other tools as required when specific parts of your bike need maintenance or replacement. However, try to follow a few general principles when using the tools.

When using tools on a bike, especially lightweight bikes, you need a delicate touch. If you are used to working on cars, then use less force when dealing with your bike. Nuts and bolts only need to be tight; if you over-tighten them, they will shear. If in doubt, buy torque gauges that accurately measure the correct level of tightness on a bike's nuts and bolts. See the component manufacturer's instructions for recommended torque settings. In fact, it is essential to keep all the instructions that come with your bike, tools, and any components you buy.

Buy the best-quality, precision-made tools. They will last for many years if you take care of them. Cheap tools will bend and become chipped, making it impossible to carry out some maintenance jobs properly. They could even damage the components that you work on.

Working with tools
When using your tools to maintain or repair your bike, give yourself plenty of room and always work in a neat, well-lit environment.

Essential tools

Start your toolkit with a multi-tool, wrenches to fit the cones, needle-nose pliers, cable cutters, a pump, and a workstand. Torx keys and Allen keys are required to work on some modern bikes.

Pumps and Workstand

Workstand

Frame-mounted pump

Shock pump

Track pump

Wrenches and Allen Keys

Wrenches 13–18mm

Allen keys 2–10mm

Torx keys

Allen key multi-tool

Wrench multi-tool

Mallet

Plastic mallet

Pliers and Cable Cutters

Needle-nose pliers (narrow)

Cable cutters

Needle-nose pliers (wide)

Drivetrain Tools

Crankarm bolt wrench

Chain whip

Crank puller

Chain tool

Cassette remover

Bottom Bracket Tools

Peg spanner

Hollow-axle cup tool

Wrench

Hollow-axle crank cap tool

Bottom-bracket remover

SPECIALTY TOOLS

Some maintenance and replacement tasks require specialty tools that you will not use very often. Other tools, such as the cable puller, are not essential but will make some jobs easier.

Cable puller

Chain measuring device

Bench vise

Torque wrench

Spoke keys and spoke ruler

Workshop principles

Four key principles govern the work you do on your bike. The first is neatness—find a place for each tool and return it there when you are finished with it. Second, do not use too much force to tighten components—the nuts and bolts of lightweight parts can easily shear. Third, remember the order in which you take components apart. Finally, keep all of your tools clean and dry.

The guidelines below provide you with general principles for some of the most common tools and operations in bike repair.

Using Allen keys

Put the long axis of an Allen key in the Allen bolt to make the key easier to use, both for repeated turns and in places where space is tight or restricted, such as putting a bottle cage on the down tube.

Use the short axis of an Allen key to make the final turn when tightening an Allen bolt—for example, on a chainring. You can also use this technique to start unscrewing an Allen bolt.

Using pliers

Use needle-nose pliers to hold cables and keep them under tension. Buy a small pair with pointed jaws for tight areas. Keep the jaws clean and grease-free. Lubricate the pivot with light oil occasionally.

Install a cable crimp onto a brake cable to stop the ends from fraying. Push the cable crimp onto the end of the cable and squeeze it flat with your pliers. If you are gentle, you can use the inside jaws of your cable cutters.

Using a wrench

Always use the correct size of wrench for the nut you are tightening or loosening. Hold the wrench firmly at the end to maximize leverage. Make sure that the jaws fully enclose the nut to prevent it from slipping.

Cutting cable housings

Cut a brake cable housing between the spirals of the metal tube under the sheath. If the spirals become compressed, squeeze them with the inside of your cutter jaws until they are round.

Cut a gear cable housing through the wire under the sheath. If you need to, squeeze the wire with the inside of your cutter jaws until its cross-section is round again.

Organizing a bike workshop

Regularly maintaining your bike and carrying out essential repairs means that you can keep your bike at peak performance. If you have the space, the best place to do this is in a workshop that is well organized and equipped with all the tools you need for your particular bike. Create a workshop that is dry with plenty of light—and follow the four key workshop principles.

Cleaning your bike

Bikes are tough but require care to keep them running efficiently. Many parts are open to the elements, coming under attack from water, mud, and grit. The latter sticks to lubricants and forms a grinding paste that can wear out moving parts. The purpose of cleaning—as well as making your bike look good—is to remove old lubricant and grit.

Cleaning also provides an opportunity to examine your bike. Look for signs of wear in all the moving parts, and check the frame, paying close attention to the underside of the main tubes, the insides of seat- and chain-stays, and the dropouts.

It does not take long to clean a bike, but the return is immense. The best results are obtained by cleaning the moving parts first, then the frame, finishing off with lubrication.

Cleaning equipment

- Stiff-bristled brushes • Bucket • Hose
- Cloth • Degreaser; detergent, bike polish

Washing off dirt and oil

1 **Remove the wheels** from the bike, and clamp the frame in a workstand or hang it up.

- Place a chain holder in the rear drop-out. This allows the chain to run freely while the wheel is removed, so that it can be cleaned thoroughly.

- Wash any excess dirt off the frame with a hose or low-pressure bike-washer. To remove old oil and grit, apply degreaser to the chainset, front and rear mechs, and the chain, covering each link.

4 **Scrub the chain** with hot soapy water. Use a specific chain-cleaning brush to get the best results. Try to remove as much old lubricant from the chain's surface as possible.

- Scrub the front and rear mechs, too.

5 **Clean the rest of the bike** with soapy water or a proprietary frame detergent.

- Use a large brush to work the cleaner inside the frame angles, and over the handlebars and brake levers. Pedals, the insides of the brake calipers, cable guides, and under the saddle and bottom bracket all need particular attention.

- Scrub the cassette and wheels with soapy water.

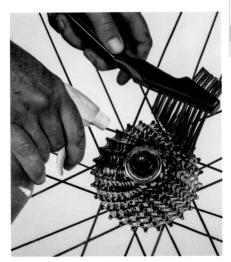

2 **Use a stiff-bristled brush** to work the degreaser into the chain links, applying more if required. Do the same with the teeth on the chainrings, and with the front and rear mechs. Use plenty of degreaser and scrub hard.

3 **Spray or brush degreaser** onto the cassette, ensuring not only to cover it, but to get plenty of degreaser between the sprockets.

• Scrub the cassette hard with a stiff, long-bristled brush to remove old lubricant and grit.

6 **Rinse the frame and wheels** with water, using a hose or low-pressure bike-washer if desired. Dry the frame with a soft cloth and check the components for wear or damage. Any cracks or dents need professional assessment.

• Depending on the extent of any wear found on the components, you can either replace them, or plan how and when to repair or maintain them.

• Bike polish gives an extra bit of sparkle to your frame, dispersing moisture and adding a protective layer to parts and components (*inset*). Be careful not to spray any on the brake pads or wheel rims.

• Give both tire treads and sidewalls a wipe down with a dry cloth, and replace the wheels.

• Now that it is clean, fully lubricate your bike (*see pp.38–9*).

Lubricating your bike

Regular lubrication helps a bike run smoothly and prevents excessive wear and tear. Each time a part of the bike is lubricated, remember to remove the old oil and grease with degreaser first (*see pp.36–7*). Applying new lubrication on top of old does not work because lubricants attract grit and dirt to the bike and form a grinding paste that can cause damage.

The lubricants needed vary from light spray oil (dry lube) and heavier oil (wet lube) to light grease manufactured specifically for bikes and anti-seize compounds.

STEP LOCATOR

Applying oil and grease

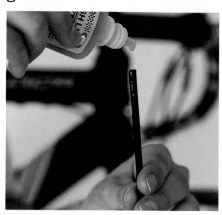

1 **Dribble some light oil** inside the cable housings before you install a new cable. This makes sure that the cable runs smoothly inside. Poor gear-shifts are often due to cables running dry inside their housings. The same is true of brakes that are hard to apply and slow to return to the ready-to-use position.

3 **Dribble light oil** onto the pivots in the front and rear derailleurs once a week. The jockey pulleys on the rear derailleur also need some light oil where they rotate around the jockey pulley bolts.

● Make sure you flush out any old oil with degreaser first.

4 **Oil the chain** after riding in wet weather, and clean, dry, and lubricate when cleaning your bike (*see pp.36–7*). Except in winter, or in bad conditions, use light oil from a spray can or bottle.

● Hold a cloth underneath the chain to catch any excess oil.

5 **Grease open bearings** after regular cleaning with a light grease specifically made for bikes. Bottom brackets and hubs need the most attention, while headsets need regreasing less often. Riding regularly in the rain shortens the interval between lubrications.

2 **Smear grease on all new cables** and, occasionally, on old ones.

• Place a blob of grease on the nipple end of the cable, then pull the cable through your thumb and index finger before installing it. Wear mechanic's disposable gloves.

6 **Spread anti-seize compound** on the seat pin and stem to prevent the two components from binding with the seat tube or steerer tube. Although you can use grease in place of anti-seize, always use a copper-based anti-seize compound for lubricating components made of carbon fiber.

Making routine safety checks

Every week or so, check the bike frame for signs of wear. Before going for a ride, run through a few checks to reduce the chances of a mechanical failure: brakes that stop working, a loose handlebar, a tire blowout, or slipping gears. The checks will help you avoid many of the accidents caused by equipment failures. Safety checks help you manage your bike, allowing for the timely replacement of parts and the completion of nonurgent maintenance work.

STEP LOCATOR

Making frame checks

1 **Inspect the frame** every week or so and look for metal fatigue. Run a finger under the down tube where it joins the head tube. A ripple in the tube's surface could lead to a break.

● Check around the area where the chainstay bridge is brazed to the chainstays, particularly on a steel frame. Cracks may form in the metal here because of the heat of the brazing process.

Making pre-ride checks

1 **Hold the front wheel** firmly between your legs and try to turn the handlebar from one side to the other. If there is any movement, check the stem and steerer bolts and tighten them if necessary.

● Try twisting the bar upward to look for rotational movement.

2 **Apply each brake** fully and push the bike forward. If the lever pulls to the bar before the brake stops a wheel from rotating, adjust the travel or replace the pads.

● Apply the front brake. Tighten the headset if you feel any play in the steerer assembly.

3 **Lift the bike,** slowly spin the wheels, and check the tires for cuts, splits, or bulges. If you find a bulge, or are in any doubt, replace the tire. Check the tire pressure.

● Remove anything stuck in the tires, as it may cause the tire to deflate (see pp.120–1).

2 **Monitor all the parts** that are riveted to an aluminum frame, especially the cable guides or the front derailleur hangers. The rivets form potentially weak areas where stresses in the metal may develop into cracks.

3 **Protect carbon-fiber frames** in areas where the cable outers touch them. Buy a self-adhesive protective patch and peel off the back. Place it on the frame, sticky side down, under the cable outer—it is very important to prevent the cable from wearing down the carbon frame. Check the patches regularly and replace them when worn.

4 **Make sure all quick-release** levers are in the locked position, and wheel nuts are tight. Look for the words "lock" and "unlock" on the levers—"lock" is outermost when the wheel is secure (see pp.118–19).

5 **Run through the gears** and make sure that they are properly adjusted. Gears that will not mesh properly after you change them can be distracting, and if you look down to see what is wrong, potentially dangerous. If the gears are correctly adjusted and the chain is still jumping, check for a stiff link.

Maintenance

Schedule the work you need to carry out on your bike by developing a maintenance timetable. The timetable on the right provides a good template, since it shows the tasks you should perform on your bike and suggests when you should do them.

Your schedule depends on how much and where your bike is ridden. A heavily used off-road bike requires attention at much shorter intervals, while a bike used for infrequent, short road journeys will need less regular attention.

However, work carried out as part of a maintenance schedule does not replace the safety checks that must be carried out before every ride (see pp.40–1), or regularly looking for danger signs (see pp.46–7). You should also check your bike and lubricate the drivetrain every time you clean it.

MAINTENANCE TIMETABLE

EVERY WEEK

DRIVETRAIN	CHECK	Chain for wear (see pp.76–9). Gear-shift performance (see pp.54–9, 60-1, 66–9). Inner cables for fraying and outer cables for wear (see pp.46–7, 54–9). Crankarms and chainring bolts for tightness (see pp.82–3).
	LUBRICATE	Oil chain (see pp.38–9). Oil jockey pulleys (see pp.68–9).
	REPLACE	
STEERING AND WHEELS	CHECK	Headset for looseness and ease of steering (see pp.104–7). Action of quick-release levers (see pp.118–19). Wheels for broken spokes and trueness (see pp.122–3). Handlebar and stem for cracks (see pp.108–11).
	LUBRICATE	
	REPLACE	
BRAKES	CHECK	Inner cables for fraying and outer cables for wear (see pp.46–7, 128–31). Pads for wear and alignment (see pp.132–7, 142–3). Hydraulic hoses for wear, kinks, or leaks (see p.47). Brake levers, arms, discs, and calipers for cracks (see pp.128–37, 140–3). Disc and caliper bolts for tightness (see pp.142–3).
	LUBRICATE	Oil-exposed cables by wiping with wet lube on a rag.
	REPLACE	
SUSPENSION	CHECK	Fork and shock exterior surfaces for cracks (see pp.154–7, 164–5). Stanchions under shock boots, if present, for cracks (see pp.152–3). Top caps, crown bolts, and shaft bolts for tightness (see pp.150–1, 154–7).
	LUBRICATE	Teflon oil on fork stanchions and shock body, and on all seals (see pp.160–1, 166–7).
	REPLACE	

EVERY MONTH

EVERY SIX MONTHS

Bottom bracket for smoothness, play, bent axle (*see pp.86–91*)
Pedals for play, and clipless pedals for play and release action (*see pp.94–7*).
Rear derailleur pivots for play (*see pp.68–9*).
Cog and chainring teeth for wear (*see pp.46, 80–1*).
Check battery levels of electronic gear systems, and recharge in accordance with manufacturer's instructions (*see pp.62-3*).

Oil derailleur pivots (*see pp.38–9*).
Oil and grease inner and outer cables (*see pp.38–9*).
Oil clipless pedal release mechanisms (*see pp.48–9*).

Chain on a heavily used bike (*see pp.76–9*).

Hubs for play on axles, roughness, or tight spots (*see pp.116–17*).
Rubber seals on hubs for splits (*see pp.116–17*).
Covers, if present, on headsets (*see pp.48–9*).

Oil the seals on hubs (*see pp.116–17*).

Discs for wear and calipers for alignment (*see pp.140–3*).

Grease inner cables and oil inside outer cables (*see pp.38–9, 128–31*).

Brake pads of heavily used mountain bikes (*see pp.134–7, 140–1*).

Fork and shock for play (*see pp.152–7, 164–5*).
Fork stanchions to see if oil line visible (*see pp.152–7*).
Fork and shock seals for cracks and slackness (*see pp.152–7, 162–3*).
(Play, absence of oil lines, and cracked seals are all evidence of worn seals, which should be replaced by a trained technician.)
Fork and shock sag (*see pp.152–3, 164–5*).

Turn bike upside down and store overnight so oil can redistribute in fork.

EVERY SIX MONTHS

Freehub body and freewheel for play (*see pp.80–1*).
Rear derailleur frame fixing bolt for play (*see pp.68–9*).
Cleats for wear (*see pp.98–9*).
Jockey pulleys for wear (*see pp.68–9*).

Oil in hub gear, if equipped with oil port (*see pp.72–3*).
Grease bearings in pedals (*see pp.94–5*).

Chain (*see pp.76–9*).
Inner and outer cables (*see pp.54–9*).
Cogs on a heavily used bike (*see pp. 80–1*).

Bearings in open-bearing hubs for wear (*see pp.116–17*).
Bearings and bearing surfaces in headsets for wear (*see pp.104–7*).

Grease open-bearing hubs (*see pp.116–17*).
Grease headsets (*see pp.104–7*).

Handlebar tape and grips (*see pp.108–11*).

Grease brake bosses (*see pp.134–7*).

Inner and outer cables (*see pp.128–31*).

Fork steerer for cracks, by removing the headset (*see pp.104–7*).

Check bushings and bearings in rear suspension for play, and lubricate them.

Fork oil (*see pp.154–7*).
Seals on forks and shocks, as part of biannual service by trained technician.

Troubleshooting

The symptoms of some of the things that can go wrong with your bike are listed in this troubleshooting chart. It explains why a bike may be showing these symptoms and then suggests a solution, referring you to the pages where you will find a detailed sequence of steps to guide you.

If you still find the problem difficult to solve, consult the How They Work pages for the specific part you are working on, so that you can understand it better. However, sometimes the symptoms confronting you can be due to a different malfunction from the one suggested in this chart. If after consulting the relevant pages in the book you still cannot solve the problem, ask the experts at a good bike shop for help.

SOLVING COMMON PROBLEM

PROBLEM

TRANSMISSION

The chain will not shift onto a smaller cog or chainring.

The chain will not shift onto a larger cog or it shifts but does not run smoothly on it.

The chain shifts cleanly, but jumps on the cogs when pressure is applied to the pedals.

The chain rubs on the inner then the outer side of the front derailleur cage. On a bike with a single chainring, the chain persistently falls off.

STEERING AND WHEELS

When you apply the front brake and push the bike forward, the headset moves forward relative to the head tube.

You hear a sudden snapping noise come from a wheel while riding and/or the wheel goes out of true.

There is side-to-side play of a hub on its axle, or when turning the axle in the hub you feel either a roughness or tight and loose spots.

When pedaling forward, the cassette spins, but there is no drive to the bike. Alternatively, the cassette spins before the drive is engaged or there is a lot of side-to-side play ir the cassette.

BRAKES

The brakes are hard to apply and/or sluggish to release.

You have to pull the brake lever a long way before the brakes engage.

The two brake pads do not contact the braking surface at the same time.

The brake pads contact the braking surface without pulling the lever too far, but are ineffective at slowing the bike.

SUSPENSION

The fork regularly reaches the limit of its travel (bottoms out

On steep, smooth descents, the rear wheel lifts under braking.

The front wheel shakes up and down when cornering.

A rear air/oil shock regularly reaches the limit of its travel (bottoms out).

CAUSE	SOLUTION
Either grit has become lodged inside the cable outers or the cable lubrication has dried up.	Strip down the cables, flush the outers with degreaser, clean the inners with degreaser, lubricate, and reassemble (see pp.38–9, 54–61).
The cable has stretched, the derailleur is misaligned, or the electronic gear-shift system is malfunctioning.	Unclamp the cable at the derailleur, pull through any slack, and tighten. Then set up the derailleur (see pp.62–3, 66–9).
Either the chain has a stiff link; or the chain or cogs, or both, are worn; or a chainring may be bent.	Check the chain for a stiff link and remove it if found. If no stiff link, replace the chain. If the problem persists, replace the cogs. If the chainring is bent, replace it (see pp.76–83).
The bottom bracket is worn or its axle may be bent.	If the bottom bracket is a cartridge type, replace it. If it is a hollow-axle bottom bracket, replace the cup and bearing units. If it is a press-fit bottom bracket, it may be possible to replace the bearings if they are worn (see pp.86–91).
The headset is loose or worn.	Strip and inspect the headset. Replace bearings if worn, regrease, and reassemble. Inspect the cups and races; if they are worn, you should let a good bike shop replace the whole headset (see pp.104–7).
A spoke may have broken.	Replace the spoke and true the wheel (see pp.122–3).
The hub bearings are worn, or in the case of tight and loose spots, the axle is bent.	Replace the bearings or the axle (see pp.116–17).
The freehub body is worn.	Replace the freehub body (see pp.80–1, 116–17).
Grit and dirt is inside the cable outers or the lubrication on the inner cables has dried.	Strip down the cables, flush the outers, and clean the inner cables with degreaser, lubricate both, and reassemble (see pp.38–9, 60–1, 128–31).
The pads are wearing down or the cable has slipped through the clamp bolt.	If the pads are not too worn, take up the extra travel by unclamping the brakes, pulling the cable through the clamp, and tightening. If the pads are worn, replace them (see pp.128–37, 140–7).
Your brakes are not centered.	Follow the procedures for centering the type of brakes on your bike (see pp.128–37).
There is grease on the pads, foreign bodies embedded in them, or they are wearing unevenly. You may even need a different compound of brake pad.	Rub the pads with emery cloth. Remove foreign bodies with long-nosed pliers. Install new pads if they are worn unevenly. Seek advice from a bike shop regarding different pad compounds (see pp.128–37, 140–7).
With air/oil forks, not enough air is in the system. With coil/oil forks, too light a spring is installed.	Pump in more air. Replace springs with heavier duty springs (see pp.152–5).
The front of the bike is diving under braking because the fork is not stiff enough.	Pump in air, or increase preload, according to the type of fork on your bike (see pp.152–5).
The fork's rebound is set too fast.	Use the relevant adjuster to reduce the speed of the fork's rebound (see pp.152–5).
Insufficient air in the shock, or too much damping, means that the shock is not returning from each compression quickly enough.	Set up the sag on the shock again. If the problem continues, use the damping adjustment to speed up the action of the shock (see pp.164–5).

Spotting danger signs

The more you ride your bike, the quicker the various moving parts, particularly tires and brake pads, will wear away. Replacing the parts as soon as they become worn not only keeps the bike running smoothly but also reduces the chances of an accident. You will save money, too, since worn parts have the additional effect of wearing out other parts.

As you run through your safety checks (*see pp.40–1*), look for worn teeth on cogs and chainrings, worn brake pads, split or frayed cables, worn wheel rims, bulging or split tires, and worn tire treads. If you spot any danger signs, take action as soon as you can. You must replace a damaged part before you next ride your bike.

Checking for wear
Regularly check the tires, rims, brakes, chainrings, cables, and cogs so that you can spot signs of wear as early as possible.

Cables and hoses

Rims and tires

Chainrings

Cogs

Brakes

Cogs and chainrings
Worn teeth

Regularly check for worn or missing teeth on a chainring or cog. The chain can jump when you apply pressure to the pedals, especially if you are out of the saddle, and you may be pitched forward and crash. Replace the chainring or cog as soon as you see this sign (*see pp.80–3*).

Brakes
Worn brake pads

Regularly check brake pads—including those on disc brakes—for uneven wear. This is a sign that they are not contacting the braking surface evenly. The effectiveness of your brakes is compromised, because not all the pad's surface is in use. Fit new pads and adjust your brakes (*see pp.132–45*).

Rims and tires

Look for evidence of deep scoring on the rims of each of your bike's wheels. Rim brakes will gradually wear out the rims, especially if you ride off-road or in winter. Eventually, the rims will fail and you could crash. Cracks around the nipples of the spokes where they join the rim are a danger sign, too. Replace the rim if you see these signs.

Worn rim

Split or bulging tire

Check the whole circumference of the tires on both wheels for bulges or splits in the tread or walls. Tires with bulges, distortions, or splits anywhere on them are likely to blow when you ride your bike. If you spot any of these failures on your tire, replace it immediately (*see pp.120–1* for how to remove and reinstall a tire).

Worn tread

Look closely at the tread of both tires for signs of wear. If the tread is worn, the tire has lost structural strength and can break down and distort or bulge. The result can be a blowout during the course of a single ride. A tire that has been skidded and lost enough rubber to develop a flat spot can also be dangerous. Replace the tire if you see either sign (*see pp.120–1*).

Cables and hoses
Split or leaking hose

Check the entire length of each brake hose—used on bikes with hydraulic brakes to carry fluid from the brake lever to the brake itself—for splits or any sign of leaking brake fluid. The evidence might be as little as a single droplet or a smear of fluid. Leakages require immediate attention from a qualified mechanic, who will be able to replace the brake hose with a new one.

Split or frayed cables

Split brake outer

Frayed gear outer

Check all cables and cable outers for signs of splitting and fraying. Frayed inner cables can snap, leaving you without gears, which is inconvenient, or without brakes, which is dangerous. Change the cable before you ride again (*see pp.54–9, 128–31*). Worn or split outers reduce the effectiveness of your brakes and allow dirt to get in and clog the cables. Change the outer as soon as you can.

Preparing for wet weather

These steps will help you prepare a bike for a rainy winter, a particularly wet climate, or if most of your riding is done off-road. The mud, sand, and water that your wheels spray up into every part of the bike combine to form a damaging, grinding paste. Salt, if used to treat roads where ice is likely to occur, will quickly corrode your bike. Regular cleaning and lubricating helps with protection, but try to stop the mud and salt from reaching the delicate parts of the bike in the first place. The overall aim when protecting a bike in wet weather is to prevent water from reaching the interior parts and washing the lubricant off the exposed parts.

Protecting a bike
Attach mudguards, insert seals, and lubricate the exposed parts to protect a bike from wet conditions.

Mudguard

Headset

Derailleur

Seat post collar

Pedal

Chain

Shielding exposed components

Sealing the seat post collar

Keep water out of the point where the seat pin enters the frame. Mark this junction and remove the pin. Pull a piece of narrow road-bike inner tube over the frame. Insert the pin through the tube to the mark and use a cable tie to secure the tube.

Sealing the headset

Place a cover over the headset to provide protection. You can attach a protector to the headset without removing any components by simply fastening the velcro.

Attaching mudguards

Fasten a mudguard to the seat pin and you will block much of the spray from the back wheel. For the front wheel, use a guard that clips onto the frame and is secured in place with cable ties. Full mudguards, which attach to the fork and rear dropout, give almost full protection for on-road biking but get clogged up off-road.

Weatherproofing the drivetrain

Cleaning and lubricating the chain

Lubricate and clean your chain as often as you do in summer and after every wet ride. Apply the same light lubricant that you use in the summer and then apply a heavier oil, which will not wash off as easily. Only coat the rollers and insides of each link with heavier oil because it attracts more dirt.

Cleaning and lubricating derailleurs

Dribble oil onto the pivots around which the front and rear derailleurs move. Use a heavier, wet oil rather than the oil you would normally apply during the summer. Every time you dribble oil like this, first flush out the old oil by dribbling some degreaser onto the pivots and letting it sink in for a few minutes.

Cleaning and lubricating pedals

Apply heavier, wet oil to lubricate the retention mechanism of clipless pedals after degreasing all the moving parts. The heavier oil will not wash off as easily as dry oil. Regularly clean off old oil with degreaser and apply new oil in order to prevent the accumulation of grit and the consequent increase in pedal wear.

MAINTAINING YOUR DRIVETRAIN

The drivetrain is the heart of your bike. Fine-tune and regularly service the system to ensure that the gear-shifters, chain, crankset, cassette, and derailleurs work together in perfect harmony.

CABLES AND SHIFTERS

Cables and shifters enable the rider to operate the gears. Cables are under constant tension and need to be replaced regularly and kept well lubricated. They must also be inspected often and replaced if they show signs of wear. Shifters require only occasional lubrication of their inner workings.

How they work

An inner cable connects the gear-shifter to the derailleur, and allows the rider to change gears. Gear-shifts made by a gear-shifter cause the front derailleur to shift the chain from one chainring to another, or the rear derailleur to shift the chain from one cog to another. Pulling the gear cable shifts the chain from a smaller to a larger chainring or cog; releasing the gear cable shifts the chain from a larger to a smaller chainring or cog. The left-hand shifter controls the front derailleur; the right-hand shifter controls the rear derailleur.

Controlling the gears
The cables and shifters on a bike allow the rider to effortlessly control the gear system.

Cable clamp
Attaches the cable to the rear derailleur

Rear derailleur
Moves the chain from one cog to another

REAR DERAILLEUR CABLE

A clamp connects the cable to the rear derailleur. When the shifter is pushed, the cable pulls the rear derailleur inward, moving the chain from a smaller to a larger cog. When the shifter releases the cable tension, the springs on the rear derailleur pull the jockey wheels, and the chain, back to a smaller cog.

Front derailleur
Moves the chain from one chainring to another

SHIFTING GEARS

In this Campagnolo shifter, the rider pushes the inner shift lever to pull the cable and move the derailleur. When the rider depresses a lever on the inner side of the lever hood, the derailleur moves back.

Gear-shifter
Pulls and releases the gear cable

COMBINED BRAKE LEVER/GEAR-SHIFTER ANATOMY

Gear-shifters are often combined with the brake levers on the handlebar. On this Shimano gear-shifter, the brake lever also acts as a shift lever. When the rider pushes the brake lever inward with the fingers, the control cable attached to it is pulled and a ratchet mechanism is lifted. A click of this mechanism equals one shift of the front or rear derailleur, which moves the chain across the chainring or cogs. The ratchet mechanism then holds the cable in its new position. When the rider pushes the inner shift lever inward, the ratchet mechanism's hold is released and the shifter's pull on the cable ceases.

Cable
Connects the shifter to the rear derailleur

Lever hood
Attaches the levers to the handlebar

Ratchet mechanism
Holds the cable

Cable inner
Controls a derailleur

Inner shift lever
Releases the cable

Cable outer
Counteracts the cable pull

Brake lever
Pulls the cable

Drop handlebar gear cables

Keeping gear cables clean and lubricated, and replacing them if they fray, is very important for smooth shifting. Change them as a matter of course at least once a year, or more often if you are a heavy user.

Lubrication reduces the effects of friction between the inner cable and the cable housing, and helps keep out water and grit. If the gears become difficult to shift to a different chainring or cog, the cable is probably dry and needs lubrication.

These steps show how to attach a new gear cable to a SRAM shifter. Attaching cables to gear shifters made by other manufacturers, such as Shimano and Campagnolo, will be slightly different, but the order of each task in the overall sequence is generally the same.

STEP LOCATOR

Parts of gear-shift units

SRAM shifter

Rubber brake hood cover

Shimano shifter

Gear-shift lever

Gear-shift lever

Gear-shift lever

Brake lever

Brake lever

Toolbox

- Allen key multi-tool • Long-nosed pliers
- Cable cutters • Oil

Replacing a SRAM gear cable

1 **Use the shifter to move the chain** to the smallest cog if you are installing a new rear-derailleur gear cable, or to the smallest chainring for a new front-derailleur gear cable.

● To do this with Shimano and SRAM shifters, move the inner shift lever toward the center line of the bike.

● To do this with Campagnolo shifters, push down on the lever situated on the inner side of the lever hoods.

4 **Insert the new, lubricated cable** into the same hole in the shifter that the old cable emerged from, pushing until you see it emerge from behind the lever hood.

● Pull the new cable all the way through the shifter until the nipple fits snugly in place.

2 **Undo the cable clamp bolt** on the derailleur, then release the old cable and push it through the guidance boss on the derailleur.

● Note the path by which the cable enters the derailleur and how it sits in the cable clamp. You must replicate this with the new cable.

● If the cable is frayed, cut off the frayed end with a pair of cable cutters to allow it to pass through the guidance boss and the outer cables.

3 **Remove the old cable** from a SRAM or Campagnolo shifter by rolling the rubber lever-hood cover forward. Push the cable from behind the shifter and watch where the cable nipple emerges from the side of the shifter hood body.

● For Shimano shifters, the cable emerges from under the hood cover without rolling it forward.

● Pull the old cable from the shifter by its nipple.

5 **Dribble a little oil into the cable outers** and insert the cable through the outers. Make sure they are firmly seated in the cable guides on the frame. If you are installing new outers, cut them to the same length as the ones they replace.

● Make sure metal ferrules are fitted to both ends of each outer.

6 **Pull the cable through** all the outers and cable guides, and reconnect it to the derailleur by tightening the cable clamp bolt.

● Refasten the cable so that it is in exactly the same position as it was when you unfastened the clamp bolt in Step 2.

● Make sure you pull the cable tight through the clamp bolt before you fasten it.

Bar-end gear cable

Triathlon and time-trial bikes are equipped with bar-end shifters, which are located on the ends of the aero bar extensions. Aero bars allow cyclists to adopt a low, aerodynamic riding position, while bar-end shifters make changing gears possible without the need to alter that position.

Bar-end shifters must be well maintained, since the shifters are farther from the front or rear derailleur than on any other type of bike, apart from a tandem. Installing new cables must also be done with care and precision. The cable outers should be short enough to allow the cables to follow as straight a line as possible, without restricting steering.

STEP LOCATOR

Parts of a bar-end gear-shift unit

Shift lever

Expanding joint | Shifter body

Tension adjuster

Lever cover

Toolbox

- Allen key multi-tool • Long-nosed pliers
- Cable cutters • Oil

Replacing a bar-end gear cable

1 **Shift the chain** onto the smallest cog or chainring, then unclamp the cable from the front or rear derailleur cable, depending on which cable you are replacing.

- Pull the gear-shift lever back, then push it forward to expose the cable and its nipple.

- If the cable nipple doesn't come out of the shifter, remove any handlebar tape from the aero bar extensions—it might be restricting the cable.

4 **Thread the cable** through the derailleur and its clamp bolt.

- While pulling the end of the cable to preserve tension in it, tighten the clamp bolt with a 5mm Allen key.

- Trim the gear cable with your cable cutters, leaving around ³⁄₈in (1cm) on the outside of the cable-clamp bolt.

2 **Pull the old cable** out of the shifter by the cable nipple.

● Grab the nipple with long-nosed pliers and pull it to get it started. Once there is enough cable to hold with your fingers, it should come all the way out by pulling.

3 **Make sure the shift lever** is pushed back all the way into the smallest cog or chainring position.

● Insert the new gear cable into the shifter at the same point where the old one came out.

● Push the cable through the shifter and first length of cable outer, then pull the end, feeding it through any additional outers until it reaches the front or rear derailleur.

5 **Crimp an end cap** onto the end of the new cable (*inset*). If cable ends are left uncovered, they can fray and look messy—an end cap will prevent that.

● Place the end cap over the cable end and use the inside edge of your cable cutters to squeeze it in place.

● Some cable cutters have notches on their inside edges to make the job easier, but the trick is to apply just enough pressure to squeeze the soft metal down onto the cable.

Straight handlebar gear cable

Taking care of and replacing the gear cables on a mountain bike is very similar to a road bike. However, mountain bikes are often subjected to harsher conditions than road bikes, as they are often ridden through dirt and mud, so the cables must be replaced and lubricated more regularly.

There are three main kinds of straight handlebar shifters: the Shimano Rapidfire, the Shimano Dual Control, and the SRAM. Replacing a gear cable is similar for them all.

STEP LOCATOR

Parts of gear-shift units

SRAM shifter
- Gear-shift levers
- Shifter cover
- Barrel adjuster

Shimano Rapidfire
- Star nut
- Gear-shift levers
- Ring clamp
- Shifter body

Shimano Dual Control
- Gear-shift lever
- Handlebar clamp
- Cable port
- Brake lever body
- Shifter body
- Brake/gear-shift lever

Toolbox

- 5mm Allen key ● Long-nosed pliers
- Cable cutters ● Cable pullers ● Tweezers

Replacing a Rapidfire gear cable

1 **Remove the cable-port cover** with a screwdriver (*inset*). Put the shifter in the smallest cog or chainring position.

● Unclamp the cable-clamp bolt on the derailleur, then pull the cable housing away from the barrel adjuster on the shifter. Push the inner gear cable out of the shifter so that the nipple emerges.

● Check the route of your existing cable and follow it when installing a new cable in Step 4.

3 **Cut both the cable** and cable outers with your cable cutters to the same length as the old ones you have removed. Make the outers long enough to allow the cable to travel freely inside.

● Dribble a drop of oil down each cable outer.

● Fit a ferrule to the end of each cable outer to ensure that it fits tightly into the frame's cable guides (see *pp.34–5*).

Replacing a SRAM gear cable

2 **Insert the end of the new,** lubricated cable into the hole where the cable nipple sits inside the shifter.

● Push the cable into the hole until its end shows through the barrel adjuster on the outside of the shifter body.

● Thread the cable through the first length of lubricated cable outer.

1 **For the rear cable,** put the shifter into the smallest cog. For the front cable, put the front shifter into the smallest chainring. Remove the old cable from the derailleur, then undo the star nut that holds the shifter cover in place.

● Grab the cable nipple with tweezers and remove it. Insert a new one through the barrel adjuster and seat the nipple into position. Pass the cable through the outers and reattach it to the derailleur.

4 **Thread the inner cable** through each length of outer cable.

● For a rear derailleur, unscrew the barrel adjuster to about half its range and insert the inner cable. For a front derailleur, insert the cable into the clamp.

● Pull hard with your cable pullers and tighten the cable clamp. Cut off any excess cable.

Replacing a Dual Control gear cable

1 **For the rear cable,** put the shifter into the smallest cog. For the front cable, put the front shifter into the smallest chainring.

● Open the cable port to reveal the old cable inside the shifter, and remove it with long-nosed pliers.

● Push the cable into the cable port until the cable nipple sits in the cradle inside the body.

● Follow Step 4 of Replacing a Rapidfire gear cable.

Internal cable routing

Internally routed cables—gear or brake cables that travel inside the hollow tubes of a bicycle frame—improve bike aesthetics and aerodynamics. Internal routing also protects cables from the elements, extending their life. However, internally routed cables can be tricky to replace unless you follow this simple step-by-step method. Be careful to work methodically, think carefully about each step before you undertake it, and, most importantly, do not try to rush the job. This sequence shows a gear cable being replaced, but the method works just as well for replacing brake cables.

A length of thin plastic tubing, which can be bought from good bike shops, is essential for this task. It will allow you to insert the new inner cable inside the bicycle frame and, crucially, to push it out again without the cable being lost inside the frame.

Make sure you buy a length of tubing that is wide enough for both brake and gear cables to pass through, since brake cables have a greater diameter. You will need to cut different lengths of this tubing for different cable replacements, so make sure you buy enough tubing for several jobs.

STEP LOCATOR

Toolbox

- 5mm Allen key ● Length of plastic tubing
- Electrical tape ● Cable cutters ● Pliers

Replacing internally routed cables

1 **Measure the thin plastic tubing** against the frame to gauge the length of the internal cable run. In this example, the internal run is from near the top of the down-tube to underneath the bottom bracket.

● Cut the thin plastic tubing to the length required plus 4in (10cm), to ensure that you have spare at either end when it is in position. The extra tubing makes inserting the new cable easier.

4 **With the inner cable still in place,** make sure there is an equal length of plastic tubing emerging from the holes in the frame at both ends of the internal cable run.

● Clean off any dirt or lubricant on the frame to allow good adhesion, then fix the lower end of the plastic tubing to the frame with electrical tape.

● Tape the upper end of the thin plastic tubing to the cleaned frame (*inset*).

2 **With the rear mech** in the smallest sprocket position, use the cable cutters to cut off the cable tidy at the end of the old cable.

• Undo the cable-fixing clamp on the rear mech with a 5mm Allen key, then carefully pull the cable out of the rear mech. Take out the length of cable outer from the rear mech, and remove the inner cable from any cable stops, letting it hang loosely. Do not remove it from the bike.

3 **Lubricate the length** of plastic tubing you cut in Step 1 and slide it over the end of the old inner cable.

• Push the plastic tubing up the inner cable and into the frame. If the entry point is narrow, rotate the plastic tubing slightly to help it enter the frame.

• Continue pushing the tubing until it emerges at the other end of the internal cable run. Do not remove the old cable at this point.

5 **Once both ends** of the plastic tubing have been firmly secured to the frame, remove the old cable from inside the tubing.

• Remove the old cable from the gear shifter, then insert a new inner cable (see pp.54-9).

• When that has been done, and any outers have been replaced, insert the new inner cable into the upper end of the thin plastic tubing. Keep pushing until it emerges at the other end of the tubing.

6 **Once the entire** inner cable has passed through the internal run, remove the tape holding down each end of the thin plastic tubing, sliding it out of the frame and off the new cable.

• Push the inner cable through the rear-mech cable outer, and through the cable-fixing clamp. Hold the cable under tension by pulling on the end of it with your pliers, then fully tighten the clamp.

Electronic gear shifters

It took some time to refine electronic gear shifting, but the systems available today from the major manufacturers—Shimano, SRAM, and Campagnolo—work perfectly. They represent a big step up in bike performance, provided they are well maintained.

Electronic gear systems shift the chain between sprockets and chainrings in the same way that mechanical, cable-controlled systems do. The only differences are that the shifts are signaled electronically, and each mech contains an electric motor to move the chain. As with cable-controlled systems, correct alignment of the rear mech has to be maintained, along with its travel and that of the front mech. If this is done, electronic shifts will always be sharp and accurate, and there is little danger of the chain being derailed.

The following steps demonstrate how to ensure accurate, consistent, and safe gear shifts for the Shimano Di2 electronic shift system, but those of other manufacturers are adjusted in a similar way, so these steps can still be used as a guideline.

The only other maintenance required with electronic gear shifting is to make sure that the battery is always kept charged. Recharging is straightforward—consult the system owner's manual for assistance.

STEP LOCATOR

Toolbox

- 2mm Allen key

Adjusting Di2 gears

1 **With your bike in a bike stand,** or with the rear wheel otherwise suspended, use the gear-shifter buttons to go through the gears— to a lower (*inset*) or higher gear, depending on where the chain is positioned—until the chain is roughly in the middle of the cassette, on either the fourth or fifth sprocket.

- At this point, the system is still in normal shifting mode.

4 **Press the button** under the control box again until the red light goes off, then shift the gears while listening to the sound of the chain on each sprocket. Shifts should be accurate with no excessive noise from the chain.

- If the shifts are not "clean" or the chain is noisy, repeat Steps 1-3 until everything is satisfactory.

- To check the battery, press any gear-shifter until the indicator on the control box illuminates (*inset*).

2 **To place the system** in adjustment mode, press the button underneath the control box until a continuous red light appears.

- The control box is usually secured beneath the stem, but on some bikes it can hang loose from the electric gear-shifter cables.

- Once the red light appears, the system is set up to make small adjustments to the alignment of the rear mech.

3 **Use the shift buttons** to move the rear mech left and right until the jockey wheels, seen from behind, are directly below the sprocket you selected in Step 1 (either the fourth or fifth) while the system was still in shifting mode.

- In adjustment mode the rear mech moves approximately 2mm for each press of the shift buttons, so you will be able to line the jockey wheels up perfectly with the chosen sprocket.

5 **With the system in normal** shifting mode, shift the chain onto the smallest chainring and the largest sprocket.

- Use the 2mm Allen key in the low gear adjuster—sometimes marked "L"—on the rear mech to align the jockey wheels with the largest sprocket.

- Use the 2mm Allen key to turn the low gear adjuster on the front mech until the inside of its cage almost touches the chain (*inset*).

6 **Shift the chain** so that it is on the largest chainring and the smallest sprocket.

- Use the 2mm Allen key in the high gear adjuster—sometimes marked "H"—on the rear mech to align the jockey wheels directly under the smallest sprocket.

- Use the 2mm Allen key in the high gear adjuster on the front mech until the outside of its cage almost touches the chain (*inset*).

FRONT AND REAR DERAILLEURS

The two derailleurs move the chain smoothly between the cogs and chainrings, but only if their travel is set up correctly. The derailleur pivots and jockey wheels must be checked for wear and lubricated. The front derailleurs must be properly aligned with the chainrings.

How they work

The front and rear derailleurs change the gears on a bike. To move up a gear, the shifter is used to pull on the cable, which causes the front derailleur to push the chain from a smaller to a larger chainring or the rear derailleur to push the chain from a smaller to a larger cog. To move down a gear, the cable is released, causing the springs in both derailleurs to move the chain to a smaller chainring or cog. Each derailleur moves around a pivot point. High and low adjusting screws ensure that the derailleurs do not push the chain beyond the largest chainring or cog, or pull it beyond the smallest. This range is called the derailleur's travel. Once its travel is set up, and provided the cable tension is sufficient, the derailleur will make a single, clean gear-shift for every click of the shifter.

Rear derailleur
Transfers the chain from one cog to another

Cable
Pushes and pulls the rear derailleur

REAR DERAILLEUR ANATOMY

To change gears, two jockey wheels transfer the chain onto a different cog. They move in the same plane as the chain and are spring-loaded to preserve the tension in the chain. Two derailleur plates enable the jockey wheels to change gear upward, while the plate spring enables the jockey wheels to change gear downward.

Derailleur plate
Transfers cable pull to the jockey wheels

Plate spring
Pulls derailleur back as cable is released

High and low adjusters
Limit the travel of the derailleur

Cable clamp
Attaches cable to derailleur plates

Cable
Pulls derailleur plates

Jockey wheel spring
Preserves the tension in the chain

Jockey wheel
Pulls and pushes the chain

Jockey wheel cage
Holds the jockey wheels

Working with the shifters
The front and rear derailleurs work in harmony with the shifters to provide easy, quick, and accurate gear-shifts whenever the rider needs them.

REAR DERAILLEUR IN USE

When the cable is pulled, it causes both the derailleur plates to swing inward on four pivot points, causing the jockey wheels to guide the chain onto a larger cog. When the cable is released, the plate spring moves the chain back to a smaller cog.

Large cog *The chain is moved to the largest cog by the pull of the cable.*

Small cog *The chain is returned to the smallest cog by the plate spring.*

FRONT DERAILLEUR ANATOMY

When pulled, the cable moves the outer arm, which acts like a lever to push the front derailleur cage away from the bike. This moves the chain from a smaller to a larger chainring. When the cable is released, a spring on the derailleur's inner arm pulls the cage back toward the bike.

High and low adjusters *Limit the travel of the derailleur cage*

Clamp bolt *Fixes derailleur to the frame*

Outer arm *Acts as a lever*

Cable clamp *Holds the cable to the derailleur*

Pivot point *Acts as a fulcrum for the arm*

Derailleur cage *Moves the chain*

Chainring *Engages the chain*

Chainring *Carries the chain*

Front derailleur *Transfers the chain from one chainring to another*

Front derailleur

Front derailleurs shift the chain from one chainring to the next. There are two main kinds: braze-on derailleurs (*below*) are fixed by an Allen bolt to a lug, or protrusion, on the bike frame; band-on derailleurs are attached to a band that goes around the frame and is part of the derailleur.

There are two important maintenance jobs for a front derailleur: setting it up after installing a new control cable and adjusting it when it is not shifting properly. You should also clean the derailleur regularly to prevent the buildup of dirt, which interferes with its operation and will quickly wear it out.

For the derailleur to work perfectly, the lower edge of the derailleur cage's outer side should be no higher than 2mm above the largest chainring. The cage's outer side must also be parallel with the chainrings.

Correct shifts depend on the front derailleur's traveling a certain distance per shift. High and low adjusting screws on the derailleur will control this travel.

STEP LOCATOR

Parts of a braze-on front derailleur

Cable-fixing clamp
Pivots
Front derailleur cage (outer side)
High/low adjusters
Frame-fixing clamp
Front derailleur cage (inner side)

Toolbox

- Needle-nose pliers • 5mm Allen key
- Screwdriver • Cable cutters

Adjusting a front derailleur

1 **Shift the chain** onto the largest cog and the smallest chainring.

- Pull the front derailleur cage away from the frame. The lower edge of its outer side should clear the largest chainring by 2mm. If it is more or less, undo the frame-fixing clamp and raise or lower the front derailleur.

- Line up the cage parallel with the chainrings and tighten the frame-fixing clamp.

3 **Pull the gear cable** through the cable clamp and tighten the cable-clamp bolt.

- Cut off any excess cable with your cable cutters and put on a cable crimp (*see pp.34–5*).

- Repeat Steps 2 and 3 if, after a couple of rides, the chain will not shift up to the next chainring, since cables can sometimes stretch slightly.

2 **Undo the cable–fixing** clamp until the cable comes free.

● Look for the low gear adjuster (usually marked "L") and screw it in or out until the inner side of the front derailleur cage is about 2mm from the chain. You have now set the starting point of the derailleur's travel.

● Take this opportunity to clean the guide in which the cable runs under the bottom-bracket shell. Use degreaser, and then wash and dry the whole area.

● Put a little dry lubricant in the guide.

4 **Shift the chain** across until it is on the smallest cog and the largest chainring.

● Repeat Steps 2 and 3 if the chain will not shift onto the largest chainring.

5 **Screw in the high adjuster** (usually marked "H") to bring the outer side of the front derailleur cage to about 2mm from the chain.

● Unscrew the higher adjuster to allow more travel if, when you shift to the largest chainring, the chain does not move onto it.

● Check the action by shifting a few times between all the chainrings.

Rear derailleur

Most rear derailleurs are indexed, which means that for every click of the shifter, either up or down, the derailleur will shift the chain from one cog to the next.

Occasionally, you may find that the chain does not quite move onto the next cog when you make a single shift, or else it skips a cog in an overshift. In either case, the rear derailleur needs to be adjusted. You will also need to follow the steps in this sequence whenever you fit a new cable (*see pp.52–9*).

To ensure that the rear derailleur works faultlessly, pay particular attention to its jockey pulleys because this is where oil and dirt can accumulate. Degrease and scrub them every time you clean your bike (*see pp.36–7*). Whenever you lubricate the jockey pulleys or the rear derailleur pivots, make sure you wipe off any excess oil.

STEP LOCATOR

Parts of a rear derailleur

Barrel adjuster

Jockey wheel

Derailleur pivot

Cable-fixing clamp

Jockey cage

Toolbox

● Needle-nose pliers ● Cable cutters
● 5mm Allen key ● Screwdriver

Adjusting a rear derailleur

1 **Shift the chain** onto the biggest chainring and smallest cog, then undo the cable-fixing clamp so that the cable hangs free.

● Check the cable and install a new one if it shows any sign of fraying.

● Screw the barrel adjuster in or out, until it is at half of its range.

4 **Shift back to the smallest cog,** then shift upward through each gear. If the rear derailleur does not shift all the way onto the next-biggest cog, screw out the barrel adjuster until it does. If the derailleur overshifts and skips a cog, screw in the barrel adjuster until it stops.

2 **Use the high** adjuster (usually marked "H") to line up the jockey pulleys with the smallest cog.

● Once you have lined them up, rotate the pedals forward while adjusting the "H" adjuster until the chain runs smoothly.

● Pull the cable downward through the cable-fixing clamp and reclamp it.

3 **Shift onto the smallest chainring** and largest cog.

● Push the rear derailleur with your fingers toward the spokes. If it moves beyond the largest cog, screw in the low adjuster (marked "L") until the derailleur stops at the largest cog.

● Turn the pedals to see if the chain runs smoothly. If it does not, adjust the "L" in or out.

5 **Prevent the jockey pulleys** from making contact with the bigger cogs by screwing in the adjuster that butts onto the rear derailleur hanger on the frame dropout. Remember to make this adjustment if you install a block or cassette with bigger cogs than usual.

HUB GEARS

Hub gears located inside the hub casing alter the speed at which the back wheel revolves. They require little routine maintenance, and since they are sealed, most hub gear systems do not need to be lubricated regularly. The control cables must still be inspected regularly and replaced if they are worn.

How they work

All hub gears work according to the same basic principle. A system of internal cogs makes the hub casing, and therefore the rear wheel, turn at a different speed from a single, external cog that is driven by the pedals via the chain. The external cog is connected to the internal cogs by a driver unit, and the cogs rotate the hub casing at different speeds. Spokes attach the casing to the rim, thereby turning the rear wheel.

A shifter on the handlebar operates a mechanism attached to the hub. This mechanism causes various combinations of different-sized cogs within the hub to engage with a ring gear, which drives the hub casing. Each combination gives a different gear ratio, and the number of gears depends on the number of cogs within the hub.

SHIMANO HUB GEAR ANATOMY

To change gears, the rider activates the shifter to pull the cable, which turns the satellite on the drive side of the hub. This triggers a mechanism within the driver unit to move two carrier units containing cogs. Different cogs are brought into contact with the ring gears. When the cable is released, the spring-loaded carrier units move the cogs back to a different combination.

Hub casing
Turns the wheel

Cable and satellite
Side view of the hub

Bearings
Aid the rotation of the hub casing

Driver unit
Transfers the cog's drive and causes the carrier unit to engage different cogs with the ring gear

Carrier unit
Carries the different-sized cogs

Ring gear
Turns the hub casing

Protecting the gears
The hub gear mechanism is
fully enclosed to protect it
from damage, dirt, and water.

Hub gear unit
*Contains the cogs that
allow gear changes*

Hub gear

If the cable to your hub gear snaps or shows any signs of wear, you must replace it. Although there are several different makes and models of hub gears, all with subtle differences in the way they work, replacing a gear cable is similar to the Shimano Alfine pictured here. The main difference between them is the way the cable couples with the shift mechanism, but each have some form of connector that requires loosening, like the cable-clamp bolt pictured here.

Removing a hub-gear wheel is necessary for installing a new tire or mending a puncture, and requires a different procedure from that for bikes with derailleur gears. The other main maintenance demand is regular lubrication—most hub gears have an oil port through which oil can be dribbled.

STEP LOCATOR

Parts of a hub gear

Cog   Cable outer

Gear satellite   Cable-joint stopper

Cable-clamp bolt

Toolbox

● Wrenches to fit cable-clamp bolt and wheel-axle nuts ● Measuring tape

Replacing a hub-gear cable

1 **Click the gear-shifter** so that the chain moves into first gear. This is to remove tension from the gear cable.

● The cable operates a mechanism on the hub called the satellite, which initiates each gear change. Take hold of the satellite and twist it counterclockwise (*inset*).

3 **Measure the distance** from the cable-clamp bolt to the last length of cable outer. You will need this measurement for Step 4.

● Place a wrench on either side of the cable-clamp bolt, then loosen the bolt. Remove the bolt from the old cable.

● Push the old cable through any other lengths of cable outer, then remove it from the shifter.

The top right shows "Hub gear 73"

Removing the rear wheel

2 Unhook the cable and the cable-clamp bolt from the gear satellite, then let the satellite return to its resting position.

- You need both hands to do this—one to turn the gear satellite clockwise, and the other to remove the clamp bolt.

1 Select first gear and detach the cable and its outer from the cable-joint stopper, moving them outward to unhook them.

- Unhook the cable and clamp bolt from the gear satellite as in Step 1 and 2 of Replacing a hub-gear cable.

4 Insert the new cable into the shifter and feed it through any lengths of cable outer to the hub gear.

- Thread the new cable through the cable-clamp bolt. Position the bolt the same distance from the cable outer as the measurement you took in Step 3, then tighten it.

- Reverse Step 2 to hook the cable-clamp bolt back in place.

2 With a wrench on each wheel nut, undo the wheel nuts on each side of the hub that hold the hub in the frame.

- Lift the rear wheel backward and up, then lift the chain from the cog.

- Reverse Steps 1 and 2 to replace the wheel.

CHAIN, CASSETTE, AND CRANKSET

With every turn of the pedals, the chain, cassette, and crankset are put under strain. The parts are in continual contact, and the motion of pedaling inevitably leads to wear. No matter how well you take care of each part, they will eventually need to be removed and replaced.

How they work

The chain, cassette, and crankset combine to form the heart of the transmission, the part of the bike through which a rider's pedal power is transferred into forward motion. The pedals drive the crankset and, via the chain, turn a cog attached to the hub of the rear wheel, which in turn rotates the wheel.

Bikes with derailleur gears use derailleurs to shift the chain onto different-sized cogs and chainrings, which make up the cassette and crankset. Each combination of chainring and cog provides a different gear ratio, potentially giving up to 33 different gears that can be used to tackle anything from steep climbs to gentle flats.

Cogs
Driven by the chain

Chain
Feeds through jockey wheels

Rear derailleur
Shifts the chain across the cogs

EXPLODED CASSETTE

The cassette transfers the motion of the chain to the wheel. It consists of cogs that slide onto the cassette body, which is bolted onto the hub. The cassette body houses the freewheel, which allows the wheel to turn when the cassette is stationary.

Cassette body
Contains the freewheel

Quick-release lever
Locks wheel into place

Lockring
Holds cogs on the body

Cog
Slides onto cassette body

Profile
Secures cogs to cassette body

Hub flange
Spokes connect hub to wheel rim

Spacer

CHAIN ANATOMY

The chain is the key to transforming pedal power into forward motion.

To transfer power efficiently, the chain must be strong, but flexible enough to fit securely around the teeth of the chainrings and cogs. To achieve this, a series of links articulate around joining pins, which are surrounded by revolving metal barrels.

Joining pin
Connects inner and outer links

Barrel
Sits between teeth of chainrings and cogs

Outer link
Shaped to allow quick gear-shifts

Inner link
Rotates around the barrel

Rear wheel
Driven by the cogs

Crankset
Powered by pedaling

Chainring
Carries the chain around the crankset

Pedal
Transmits energy to the crankset

Chain
Transmits power from the crankset

Lightweight components
The chain, cassette, and crankset are lightweight items that use the latest design and construction techniques to maximize strength and durability while maintaining an aerodynamic profile.

Chains

Replacing a chain is a regular maintenance task. All chains eventually wear out, even if you clean and lubricate them properly. A worn chain, in addition to being inefficient, will quickly wear out other transmission parts, and thus prove expensive. To determine how much a chain has worn, either use a specialized gauge from a bike shop or measure the length of 24 links. If the length is greater than 12in (300mm), the chain is worn.

New chains on derailleur gear systems are linked with a joining pin that comes with the chain. Or you can use a master link—effectively a two-part outer link that connects two inner links. The thicker chains of hub gears, BMX bikes, and some fixed-gear bikes are joined by split links (*see p.79*).

STEP LOCATOR

Parts of a Shimano chain and master link

Shimano chain

Inner link

Outer link

Pin

Master link

Outer link

Pin

Outer link

Toolbox

- Chain-link extractor
- Long-nosed pliers

Replacing a derailleur chain

1 **Shift onto the smallest chainring and cog** so that the chain is slack.

- Place a link in the link extractor and push out the pin until the chain breaks.
- Remove the old chain with the link extractor.

3 **Remove the excess links** from the end opposite from the one on which there is a joining link. Leave an inner link so that the two ends can be joined together.

- Join the chain by pushing the pin of the joining link through the opposite inner link with the extractor tool.

Using a master link

2 **Thread a new chain** through the jockey wheels and around the biggest chainring and smallest cog.

• Pull the ends of the chain together so that there is a little tension in the jockey wheels. This establishes the length of chain you need.

1 **Follow Step 2** of Replacing a derailleur chain to thread the chain through the derailleurs and around the cogs and chainrings.

• Remove any excess links with a chain-link extractor, making sure that both ends of the chain terminate with an inner link.

• Place the pin from each half of the master link into the inner links on each end of the chain.

4 **Loosen any stiff links** that occur when the chain links are compressed during Step 3.

• Flex the stiff links with a little sideways pressure until they become loose (*inset*).

• Remove the protruding part of the pin after joining a Shimano chain, as these have an extra-long joining pin.

• Break off the excess with long-nosed pliers.

2 **Pull the two ends** of the chain toward each other and loop each plate over the two pins (*inset*), then let go.

• The tension of the chain will draw the two halves of the master link back to the pins, seating them correctly and holding the chain together.

Fixed-gear transmission

The beauty of the fixed-gear bike is that it requires very little maintenance, except for regular lubrication and safety checks. Some fixed-gear bikes have a "flip-flop" rear hub, which means that there is a single cog on either side of the hub. One is a fixed gear, which forms a "direct drive" between the pedals and cog. This means that if the pedals turn, so does the rear wheel, and vice versa. The other cog is a freewheel, meaning that the rider can stop pedaling and the rear wheel will still turn.

You need to know how to remove the rear wheel in order to switch cogs. It's also useful to know how to attach fixed-gear chains, which use a split link.

STEP LOCATOR

Parts of a split-link chain

Split-link pins

Groove

Split-link chain

Outer plate

Inner links

Split pin

Toolbox

- Wrenches to attach wheel nuts
- Screwdriver (optional) • Long-nosed pliers

Swapping a flip-flop wheel

1 **Undo the rear wheel nuts** with a wrench on each one, turning both counterclockwise.

- Once the wheel is loose in the drop-outs, push it forward to create slack in the chain, then lift the chain off the cog (*inset*).

- Remove the wheel from the drop-outs by lifting it backward.

3 **Pull the wheel backward** in the drop-outs until there is just a little bit of slack in the chain.

- Finger-tighten the two wheel nuts (also known as "track nuts") that hold the wheel in place.

- Test the slack by lifting the chain with a screwdriver or wrench—there should be no more than 3/16in (4mm) of movement up and down.

Joining a split-link chain

2 **Remove the chain** from the crankset, then turn the wheel over to swap to the alternative gear—from the fixed gear to the freewheel, or vice versa.

● Hook the chain over the chosen cog, return the wheel to the bike, then replace the chain on the crankset.

1 **Join the chain** by pressing the side of the split link with the pins fixed in its plate through the two inner-link ends of the chain.

● Press the other plate onto the pins that are now sticking through the inner links.

4 **Carefully tighten** the wheel nuts, making sure that the wheel stays centered in the bike frame.

● To do this, turn the wrenches at the same time on each side, preserving the wheel's position in the drop-outs by avoiding any forward or backward pressure on the wrenches.

● Repeat the screwdriver lift in Step 3 to make sure the chain tension is still correct.

2 **Push the split pin** into the grooves of the split-link pins. These are sticking through the outer plate that you have just attached. The split pin's open end should face the rear of the bike.

● Fix the split pin in place by pushing it home with long-nosed pliers until you feel it click.

Cassette and freewheel

The cassette and freewheel allow the rear wheel to rotate while the pedals remain stationary. Their internal mechanisms—the freehub body of a cassette and the block in a freewheel—will eventually wear out and need to be replaced. The cogs on both can also wear down. These parts will also need to be removed whenever you replace a broken spoke on the drive side of the rear wheel.

The tools for removing a freewheel and a cassette depend on the manufacturer of the part that is installed on the bike. Usually, the manufacturer's name is stamped on the component. However, if you are in any doubt about which tool you need, take the wheel to the bike shop when buying a remover tool.

STEP LOCATOR

1
2
3
1-**2**-**3**

Parts of a freewheel and a cassette

Cog

Freewheel mechanism

Cogs

Inner side ridges of cassette

Freewheel

Lockring

Cassette

Toolbox

- Wrenches • Cassette remover • Chain whip
- Block remover • Grease

Removing a cassette

1 **Remove the quick-release skewer** from the rear wheel.

- Insert the cassette remover into the teeth of the lockring at the center of the cassette.

- Replace the quick-release skewer to secure the cassette remover.

Removing a freewheel block

1 **Remove the quick-release skewer** and insert the block remover into the teeth at the block's center.

- Lock the block remover in place by replacing the quick-release skewer.

2 **Wrap the chain whip** around a cog, and place the wrench on the remover.

● Press downward on both tools. This holds the cassette, while the remover unlocks the lockring.

● Remove the quick-release skewer once the lockring starts turning.

● Continue to unscrew the lockring with the cassette remover.

3 **Take off the smallest cog** after you have removed the lockring. On many cassettes, the remaining cogs come off in one piece. If they do not, you must put individual cogs back in a certain way. Failure to do so will affect the precision of gear-shifts. Usually, the cogs are marked, so that lining up these marks ensures the correct cog orientation.

2 **Put the wrench** on the flats of the block remover and turn counterclockwise.

● As the block begins to move, remove the quick-release skewer and continue turning until the block comes off.

3 **Check the integral freewheel mechanism,** which is independent of the hub. Replace it with a new block if it is worn.

● Coat the threads of the hub with grease, then screw the block on by hand.

● Lock the block in place by tightening it with the wrench and the block remover.

Cranksets

Removing a crankset is a useful skill to have because it will allow you to replace an old crank, clean or replace a worn chainring, or work on the bottom bracket.

Cranksets are attached in one of four ways. Those on a hollow-axle bottom bracket can be removed with a specialized cap-bolt tool (see Steps 1 and 2). Cranksets with a self-removing Allen bolt can be detached with an 8mm Allen key (see Step 3). Versions with a standard Allen bolt can be detached with the relevant Allen key (see Step 4). Older cranksets with a hexagonal bolt can be removed with a crankset socket wrench.

When reinstalling a crankset, keep grease or oil from touching the axle. The crankset must be dry when attached to the axle or it will work loose. After installation, go for a short ride and then try the axle bolt again. If it is slightly loose, you should tighten it.

STEP LOCATOR

Parts of a crankset

Right-hand crank

Spider

Chainring bolt

Chainrings

Toolbox

● Cap-bolt tool and rubber mallet, crank extractor, or 8mm Allen key ● 5mm Allen key
● Chainring-bolt peg-spanner

Removing a crankset

1 **For cranksets with a hollow-axle** bottom bracket, undo the left-hand crank cap bolt with a specialized cap-bolt tool.

● Insert the plastic head of the tool into the cap, using your fingers to grip the head's serrated edge. Turn the tool counterclockwise.

● Be careful as you remove the cap bolt, which is plastic and can easily be damaged.

4 **Use a long-handled Allen key** if there is an Allen bolt holding the crankset on your bike. Usually, an 8mm key is the size required.

● Work from below the crankset so that if you slip, the chainring teeth will not injure you.

● To remove the crankset, go to Step 5.

Use an Allen key to loosen the crank pinch bolt. After a few turns, the crank can be pulled off the bottom-bracket axle—pull the crank toward you to leave the axle exposed.

● Hold the right-hand crank and give the exposed end of the bottom-bracket axle a sharp tap with a rubber mallet. The crankset will come away with the axle attached.

● To remove the chainrings, go to Step 6.

Unscrew a self-removing Allen bolt with an 8mm Allen key. These kinds of bolts extract the crankset as you unscrew them.

● Steady the crank with your free hand to give you something to push against. Work from below the crankset so that if your hand or the wrench slips, the chainring teeth will not injure you.

● To remove the chainrings, go to Step 6.

Use a crank extractor to remove the crankset if it is not the self-removing type. Make sure that the washer beneath the bolt has also been removed.

● Carefully screw the extractor into the delicate threads at the center of the crankset. When the extractor is fully in, turn its handle clockwise to pull off the crankset.

● To remove the chainrings, go to Step 6.

Remove the chainrings with a 5mm Allen key on one side and a chainring-bolt peg-spanner to hold the bolt on the other. You can do this without taking the crankset off the axle, but you must remove it if you are working on the inner rings of some triple cranksets.

● Fix a creaking noise from the crankset by putting grease on the threads of the chainring bolts before you reassemble the crankset.

BOTTOM BRACKETS

There are three main types of bottom brackets: cartridge-bearing, hollow-axle, and press-fit. All use sealed bearings, which can wear out over time. If this happens on the cartridge version, replace the whole unit, but for the other types you only need to replace the bearings.

How they work

The bottom bracket joins the crank of each pedal to an axle, which rotates in the bike's frame. Each type of bracket consists of an axle, two bearings, and two cups (known as either the free cup and fixed cup, or the non-drive and drive-side cup). With the cartridge type, both cranks bolt onto the axle, but with the hollow-axle type, the drive-side crank is fixed to the axle and only the non-drive-side crank can be bolted on. The press-fit bottom bracket is just that—it is pressed inside the bottom-bracket shell with a specific tool to create a very tight fit. In engineering circles, this is called an interference fit.

Providing strength
The axle and bearings of the bottom bracket need to be both strong and reliable enough to bear the weight and power of the rider.

CARTRIDGE-BEARING BOTTOM BRACKET ANATOMY

Each of the cartridge bearings is composed of ball bearings, which are sandwiched between an inner and outer race by plastic seals. The cartridge bearings are located close to each end of the bottom-bracket axle. A tubular sleeve fits over the two bearings, filling the space between them. The fixed and free cups fit over this sleeve to create a totally sealed unit.

Fixed cup
Holds the bottom bracket in place

Outer race
Houses the bearings

Ball bearing
Supports the axle

Axle
Connects the cranks and rotates in the bearings

Free cup
Screws into the bike's frame

Crank
Turns the axle

HOLLOW-AXLE BOTTOM BRACKET ANATOMY

The drive-side crank is permanently fixed to the axle, which passes through both cups. The non-drive-side crank slides onto the axle and is secured by two pinch bolts. The crank cap bolt inserts into the end of the axle to hold the crank against a cartridge bearing, ensuring there is no play, much like the stem cap bolt on a threadless headset (see p.104).

Pinch bolts
Hold crank in place on the axle

Crank cap bolt
Presses crank against bearings

Cartridge bearing
Lets the axle turn

Cup
Holds bearings in the frame

Crank
Turns the axle

Cup
Holds the bearings in place in the frame

Axle
Connects the cranks together and rotates in the bearings

Crank
Turns the axle

Cartridge-bearing bottom bracket
Allows the smooth rotation of the axle

Cartridge bottom bracket

Cartridge bottom brackets require no routine maintenance. Their bearings are sealed from the elements—even from the water you use for hosing or pressure-washing your bike, provided that you turn the pedals forward during the wash.

When the bearings do eventually wear out, you will have to replace the whole unit. The remover tools for this job are specific to each particular bottom bracket, so check which brand is installed on your bike before buying the tools.

If you are planning a replacement, there are three types of bottom bracket axles to choose from: square-tapered, Shimano Octalink, and Isis. The type used in the steps in this sequence is square-tapered; the type shown below is Octalink.

Finally, if you are having any problems installing a bottom bracket on your bike, ask the experts at a bike shop to help you.

STEP LOCATOR

Parts of a cartridge bottom bracket

Drive (fixed-cup) side

Non-drive (free-cup) side

Bottom-bracket axle

Toolbox

- Measuring calipers • Ruler • Wrench
- Cartridge bottom bracket remover • Grease

Installing a cartridge bottom bracket

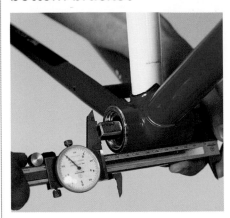

1 **Put the bike on a workstand** and remove the chainset (*see pp.82–3*).

• Use a pair of calipers to measure the length of the old axle before you remove the bottom bracket, so that you can be sure the replacement has an axle of the same length. You need to do this because different chainsets are designed to work with different axle lengths.

4 **Grease the threads** of each side of the new bottom bracket for easier installation. The non-drive threads are sometimes referred to as the free-cup and the drive-side threads are known as the fixed cup. Do not grease the drive side of a bottom bracket with Italian threads.

2 **Measure the width of the bottom-bracket** shell with a ruler. The shell forms part of the bike's frame and will be either 2¾in (68mm) or 3in (73mm) wide. This width determines the width of the bracket unit you need to buy.

3 **Remove both the crankarms** (*see pp.82–3*), insert a bottom-bracket remover into the non-drive side of the bracket, and turn the remover counterclockwise with a wrench.

● Repeat on the other side, turning clockwise. Turn counterclockwise if your bike has an Italian-threaded bottom bracket (marked 36 x 1).

5 **Insert the bottom bracket** from the drive (fixed-cup) side using the remover tool. Fit the teeth of the tool into the indentations of the bottom bracket (*see enlargement*).

● Insert the non-drive (free-cup) side when the drive side is almost in position. Use the remover to screw it in a few turns. Fully tighten the drive side, then the non-drive side.

Hollow-axle bottom bracket

Hollow-axle bottom brackets, such as those made by SRAM, Campagnolo, and Shimano, are designed to increase bottom-bracket strength. The axle bearings screw onto the outside of the bottom-bracket shell, which houses a large-diameter axle that is hollow, light, and stronger than other axles. Since the bearings are farther apart than on other bottom-bracket designs, they encounter less torque, which increases their lifespan. But they will eventually wear out, so you will need to know how to remove and replace them. The steps can also be followed if you want to upgrade to this system.

STEP LOCATOR

Parts of a hollow-axle bottom bracket

Chainring

Axle

Combined drive-side cup and sleeve

Left-hand crank

Spacers

Non-drive-side cup

Pinch bolt

Crank cap bolt

Toolbox

● Hollow-axle cup tool ● Hollow-axle crank cap tool ● Allen key multi-tool

Installing a hollow-axle bottom bracket

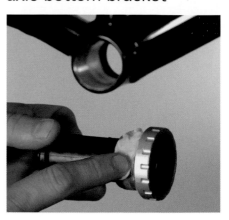

1 **The faces of the bottom bracket** shell must be flat and parallel. This requires specialized equipment, so get the frame checked at a bike shop.

● Measure the width of the bottom bracket shell, then check the manufacturer's instructions to determine how many spacers are required and which cup to put them on.

● Grease the threads of the cups and place the necessary spacers on them.

4 **Push the left-hand** crank onto the end of the axle, matching the wide notch on the axle with the wide tooth on the crank. This ensures the cranks are mounted at 180 degrees.

● Unlike other bottom brackets, a dry interface between crank and axle is not necessary. Put a little grease on the axle before you attach the crank.

● Campagnolo's hollow-axle bottom bracket fits in a similar way, but has a split axle (*inset*).

2 **Screw the cups into** the frame as far as you can with your fingers (*inset*).

- The drive-side cup screws in counterclockwise, and the non-drive-side cup screws in clockwise.

- Secure the cups on each side by tightening them with the hollow-axle cup tool (*main image*).

- Grease the axle in preparation for pushing it through the cups.

3 **Hold the drive side** (right-hand) crank and push the axle through the hole in the center of the drive-side cup.

- Continue pushing until the end of the axle pops out of the non-drive-side cup.

- You may encounter resistance, especially as you push the axle through the non-drive-side cup. If this happens, give the center of the crank a sharp tap with a plastic mallet.

5 **Grease the threads** of the crank cap bolt, and screw it into place with your fingers.

- Tighten the crank cap bolt with the crank cap tool, which draws the crank onto the axle.

- Do not overtighten the crank cap bolt. Rotate the cranks and if the axle is stiff, loosen the crank cap bolt a little.

6 **Tighten the crank** pinch bolts with an Allen key to fix the crank in place.

- The pinch bolts work as a pair, so they must be equally tight. Tighten them in sequence by screwing in the first a little, then screwing in the other by the same amount. Repeat until both bolts are tight, but do not use excessive force.

- If you have access to a torque wrench, use it to tighten the bolts to the manufacturer's instructions.

Press-fit bottom bracket

A relatively new innovation, this type of bottom bracket is lighter, simpler, and cheaper than other designs. "Press-fit" refers to the way the bearing cups and bearings fit inside the bottom-bracket shell. The cups don't screw in using shell threads, as most brackets do, but achieve an "interference" fit—an engineering term for a very tight fit—by being pressed in. The bearings are then pressed into the cups, and the axle and cranks bolt through the bearings.

Press-fit bottom brackets require little maintenance, since they are protected by good seals. Replacing the bearings is relatively easy, but requires a bearing-puller tool to remove the old set and a bearing press, or similar device, to install the new ones.

STEP LOCATOR

1　2　3　4　5　6

Parts of a press-fit bottom bracket

- Chainring
- Drive-side crank
- Drive-side axle
- Non-drive-side bearing
- Drive-side bearing
- Non-drive-side crank
- Retaining rings
- Non-drive-side axle

Toolbox

- Allen key multi-tool ● Adjustable wrench
- Bearing puller ● Bearing press ● Rubber hammer
- Circlip or snap-ring pliers, or small screwdriver

Servicing a press-fit bottom bracket

1 **Remove the chainset** using an Allen key (*inset*) or the correct tool for the crank on your bike (*see pp.82–3*).

- Remove the drive- and non-drive-side cranks from the bottom bracket.

- If the cranks have a one-piece axle, it might require a sharp knock with a rubber hammer to dislodge it from the bearings.

4 **Remove the old bearing,** which should be in place inside the bearing-puller tool.

- Repeat Steps 2 and 3 to remove the non-drive-side bearing.

- Inspect the retaining rings for damage (*inset*), and if necessary, remove and replace them using circlip or snap-ring pliers, or a small screwdriver.

- Clean the bearing cups with degreaser solution.

2 **Insert the bearing puller** behind the drive-side bearing (*inset*), making sure it doesn't snag on the retaining ring, which prevents the bearings from being inserted too far.

● There are several types of bearing-puller tools, each of which works slightly differently. In this case, a sleeve covers the bottom-bracket shell while a nut holds the bearing puller against the bearing.

● Assemble the rest of the bearing-puller tool.

3 **Thread the nut** onto the bearing puller by hand, then tighten it with an adjustable wrench to secure the bearing puller flush against the bearing.

● Using an Allen key, turn the bearing puller to extract the bearing from the drive side of the bottom bracket, while holding the nut in place with an adjustable wrench.

5 **With your fingers**, press the new drive-side bearing into the drive-side cup inside the bottom-bracket shell, making sure that you insert it straight and level into the cup.

● Insert the bearing press from the drive side.

● Press a new bearing into the non-drive-side cup, exactly as you did on the drive side.

6 **Place the non-drive-side** of the bearing press onto the central thread, tightening it up to the non-drive-side bearing with your fingers.

● Turn the bearing-press handle on the drive side until the bearings go all the way into the bottom bracket, and are flush with the face of the shell.

● Add any dust seals particular to the bottom bracket, then reverse Step 1 to refit the crankset.

PEDALS

There are two types of pedals, flat and clipless. Pedals with open bearings require regular inspection and lubrication. Clipless pedals must be lubricated to ensure easy foot release. Cleats should be correctly fitted to the rider's shoes and regularly inspected for wear.

How they work

The two pedals transfer the push from the rider's legs and feet into both crankarms, which, in turn, rotate the axle in the bottom bracket. The body of a pedal rotates around an axle and is supported on bearings that are either open or held within a cartridge. The pedal's axle screws into the crankarm.

Pedals should grip a rider's feet in some way. For example, studs that prevent foot slippage will help a rider who makes frequent stops, such as a commuter in heavy traffic. Some flat pedals are fitted with toe-clips and straps that hold the front of the foot, although they can interfere with the foot as the rider tries to remove it. Clipless pedals hold the foot securely, and release it easily whenever the rider wants.

Converting energy
Pedals are the invention that defines cycling. They are the first step in the process of converting human energy into mechanical motion.

FLAT PEDAL ANATOMY

Two bearings on the pedal's axle are held in place by a cone and lockring that screw onto the outer end of the axle. A knurled retainer attaches the pedal body to the axle. The cone (not visible) and the lockring can be adjusted to permit the free rotation of the body around the axle, without any play.

Crankarm
Transfers power to the bottom bracket

Pedal body
Rotates on the axle

Locknut
Holds the cone in place

Axle
Screws into the crankarm

Knurled retainer
Holds the body onto the axle

Ball bearings
Allow the body to rotate around the axle

Pedal
*Connects the rider's
foot to the drivetrain*

Pedal axle

The axle of a pedal is usually made from steel and the crankarms from aluminum alloy. This creates an interface where a chemical reaction can take place between the two metals, so it is important that you coat the threads with grease before you put pedals on your bike. The tools for removing the axles are specific to the brand and model of the pedals, and are either supplied with the pedals or available at a good bike shop.

Most pedals contain two bearings on which the pedal body revolves around its axle. These sometimes need to be replaced; in the case of ball bearings, they need regular cleaning, checking, and greasing.

Pedal axles can be damaged by an impact or during a fall, and a bent axle can cause riding discomfort or even injury. After removing the pedals, rotate their axles by hand, feeling for the tight spots that are evidence of a bent axle.

STEP LOCATOR

1 2 3 4 5 6

Parts of a pedal

Cleat-release mechanism

Pedal body

Pedal axle

Retainer

Wrench flats

Release tension adjuster

Toolbox

- 15mm bike wrench ● Allen key multi-tool
- Remover tool ● Degreaser ● Grease

Removing and lubricating a pedal axle

1 **Place a wrench** on the flats of the axle to remove a pedal.

● Turn the wrench counterclockwise for the right pedal, which has a right-hand thread, and clockwise for the left pedal, which has a left-hand thread.

● Steady the opposite crankarm with your hand to give you something to push against.

4 **Lift the axle from the pedal** once you have fully unscrewed the retainer nut.

● Clean the axle with degreaser and inspect it. If the axle is bent, it will need to be replaced.

● Replace the bearings on the end of the axle if they are worn.

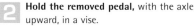

2 **Hold the removed pedal,** with the axle upward, in a vise.

● Remove the axle by using a remover tool that fits over the knurled retainer connecting the axle to the pedal.

3 **Make sure that the remover tool** fits snugly onto the retainer. The retainer may be damaged if you do not.

● Place a wrench on the flats of the remover tool in place and turn it to remove the retainer.

● Turn the wrench clockwise for the right axle retainer, which has a left-hand thread, and counterclockwise for the left axle retainer, which has a right-hand thread.

5 **Hold the cone** with one wrench and remove the locknut with another. The cone and locknut hold the bearings on the end of the axle.

● Remove the cone, then the old bearings. Clean the end of the axle.

● Set the new bearings in grease and screw the cone back on top of them. Then lock the cone with the locknut.

6 **Grease the inner bearing** to prolong its life. If it is worn, the whole axle assembly must be replaced.

● Push some grease down into the bearing after cleaning the axle. To reassemble the pedal, carry out Steps 1–4 in reverse order.

Clipless pedals

Clipless pedals were developed in response to the racing cyclist's need to apply power throughout the entire pedal revolution. They hold the foot to the pedal by locking onto a cleat attached to the sole of the shoe. The mechanism that holds the cleat is spring-loaded—the foot is released by turning the heel outward.

The release spring is an essential working part and must be kept clean and well lubricated. Use light oils on road pedals and heavier oils on off-road pedals. Wipe oil off the pedal body to stop your foot from slipping. The mechanism lets the foot pivot around its long axis during each revolution. The oil applied to the release spring is enough to keep the mechanism working well.

Toolbox
- 15mm bike wrench ● Allen key multi-tool
- Degreaser ● Stiff brush ● Oil

OFF-ROAD PEDALS

Off-road pedals are equipped with retention mechanisms on at least two sides so that the rider's feet can attach to the pedal no matter which way up it is. The pedals also let mud pass through to prevent them from becoming clogged.

Shimano off-road pedal
An open design is crucial for off-road riding to prevent the build-up of mud and dirt, which interfere with the way the pedal works. However, an open design requires regular cleaning to remove dirt and old lubricant. After cleaning, apply lubricant to the moving part of the retention mechanism. The release-tension adjuster is on the pedal's upper rear.

Top face
Retention mechanism
Pedal axle
Bottom face
Pedal body
Release-tension adjuster
Release spring

Crank Brothers pedal
This is an open design with excellent mud clearance and very few moving parts—the retention mechanism is just a simple spring. Clean the pedals regularly, and very occasionally regrease the bearings using a grease gun and a special adapter that is sold with the pedals.

Retention spring
Plan view
Axle thread
Retention bar
Retention bar
Profile view
Pedal axle
Retention spring

ROAD PEDALS

Road pedals are light, supportive, and, because of the greater speeds involved in road riding, aerodynamic. They need to engage and release the feet with equal ease, in addition to holding the foot securely. Ideally, you should be able to adjust them according to how much movement your feet make during pedaling.

Look road pedal
The Look Keo 2 Max Blade pedal uses a thin composite plate for cleat retention, rather than the coil-sprung back-plate of other Look pedals. Max Blade pedals require little routine maintenance other than regular cleaning—the spindle and bearing assembly cannot be serviced, while the release tension is altered by replacing the leaf spring.

Top face

Steel pedal protector

Bottom face

Retention mechanism

Composite release leaf-spring

Axle thread

Speedplay road pedal
The difference between Speedplay and other clipless pedals is that the release springs are located in the cleats, not in the pedal. They require little maintenance, but the release springs do wear out. A slight rocking motion when pedalling indicates that this has happened, and that they need to be replaced.

Top face

Pedal axle

Bottom face

Cleat contact

Cleat contact bolt

Pedal body

Time road pedal
These pedals offer a range of movement that can be adjusted to suit the requirements of individual riders. Keep them well maintained by scrubbing regularly with degreaser, using a stiff brush. Wash this off, then lubricate the release spring with heavier oil, dribbling it from a can.

Top face

Bottom face

Pedal body

Release spring

Release-tension adjuster

Retention mechanism

Pedal cleats

Correctly fitted cleats—positioned on the sole of your shoes to fit your own unique physiology—improve cycling efficiency and safety, and help prevent injury. They also make sure your leg muscles transfer power efficiently to the pedals, and allow you to clip your feet in and out quickly and safely.

It takes patience to set up cleats properly—do not be afraid to make adjustments later. If, after going for a ride, your foot seems to be twisting away from the position you set the cleats in, adjust the cleats until the feeling goes. But make changes in small increments.

The following steps show Look Keo road cleats, but the principles are the same for other brands, and off-road shoes and pedals.

STEP LOCATOR

Parts of a clipless pedal cleat

Cleat fixture sites

Positioning lines

Fixing screws

Cleat

Rectangular washers

Toolbox
- Flathead screwdriver or Allen keys
- Tippex or other soluble marker

Fitting a clipless pedal cleat

1 **The key to setting up cleats** is to do it according to the structure of your own foot. Put on both shoes, tighten the straps, and relax your feet inside them by wriggling your toes a little. Use a finger to feel directly behind your big toe at the widest part of your foot—this is the ball of your foot. Remember that spot.

4 **Holding the cleat parallel** to the positioning lines, fully tighten the screws so that the cleat is securely fixed to the sole of the shoe.

- Make a small mark on the outside of the shoe, level with the mid-point line on the cleat.

- Ensure that the mark can be seen when the shoe is viewed from the side.

- Repeat with the other shoe.

2 **Remove the shoe** and make a mark where the ball of your foot was.

● Once that has been done, repeat Step 1 for the other shoe. Remove that shoe and mark the position of the ball of the foot as above.

● To help with the next step, extend the mark a little bit on the sole of each shoe to form a small line. Use a marker that washes off easily.

3 **Secure the cleat** to the sole of the shoe using the screws and washers provided, but do not fully tighten them. You need to be able to move the cleat.

● Look Keo cleats, and many others, have a line marking the mid-point of their contact area with the pedals. Move the cleat so that this mark is level with the mark you made, and so the cleat's rear face is parallel to the positioning lines on the shoe's sole.

5 **You will need somebody's help** for this step. Put both shoes on and tighten the straps.

● Sit on the saddle with your bike leaning against a wall, and engage both shoe cleats in the pedals. Back-pedal so that the cranks are at the 3- and 9-o'clock positions.

● The mark on each shoe should be directly above the pedal axle (its center). Ask your helper to check the position of the mark for both shoes.

6 **If the mark** is not above the pedal axle, more adjustment is required. Undo the fixing screws and move the cleat forwards if the mark was in front of the pedal axle, or backwards if the mark was behind. Keep the cleat parallel with the sole's positioning lines.

● Repeat Step 5 to check the cleat alignment.

● Finally, loosen the screws and adjust the cleat angle if you feel your foot is twisting out or in.

4

STEERING AND WHEELS

Steering gives you control of a bike's handling and direction. Regularly check and maintain the headset, handlebar, wheels, and hubs to safeguard their reliability at all times.

HEADSETS

A headset allows the bike to be steered. The headset must be properly adjusted to allow smooth, safe steering and to prolong its life. The bearings and bearing surfaces need regular inspection and lubrication, and anything that is worn must be replaced at once.

How they work

The main function of the headset is to enable the rider to change the direction of the front wheel under any conditions. There are two types of headsets, threaded and threadless, and both hold the front fork securely in the head tube, while simultaneously allowing the fork to turn freely.

   The headset rotates on bearings, which are held in place by cups, one above the head tube, the other below. For the forks to turn freely, these two cups press on the bearings just enough to prevent any play in the part of the fork known as the steerer tube. The way this pressure (also known as load) is achieved varies between the threaded and threadless headsets.

THREADLESS HEADSET ANATOMY

The stem cap bolt at the top of a threadless headset screws into a star washer below. Some types of threadless headsets contain a wedge instead of a star washer. When the stem cap bolt is turned with an Allen key, it pushes the stem and spacer down onto the bearings in both the top and bottom cups, and pulls up the steerer tube at the same time. This places sufficient load on the bearings for the fork to turn freely with no play. The stem is secured in place on the steerer by tightening two clamp bolts (not visible on the illustration).

Stem clamp bolts
Clamp stem to steerer tube

Star washer
Grips the steerer tube

Stem cap bolt
Pulls the steerer tube upward

Stem
Links handlebar and headset

Spacer
Sits on top of the bearings

Top cup
Loads the bearings

Top bearings
Allow the steerer tube to turn in the headset

Bottom cup
Loads the bearings

Steerer tube
Connects the fork to the headset

Bottom bearings
Allow the fork to turn

Fork crown
Turns the fork

THREADED HEADSET ANATOMY

Screwing the top cup down the thread of the steerer places a load on the top bearings to the point where the forks turn freely but without play. The cup, and consequently the front fork, is then locked in place by a lockring that also screws down the threaded steerer. The stem is attached to the headset by tightening the stem's expander bolt, which pulls up a wedge and jams the stem's quill inside the threaded steerer.

Stem
Links the handlebar and headset

Quill
Fits inside the threaded steerer

Expander bolt
Draws up the wedge

Lockring
Locks the top cup in place

Top bearings
Allow the steerer to turn in the headset

Top cup
Loads the bearings

Handlebar
Steers the front wheel

Threaded steerer
Connects the headset to the fork

Wedge
Jams the quill in the steerer

Bottom bearings
Allow the fork to turn

Headset
Holds the fork in the head tube

Fork
Holds and turns the front wheel

Steering effectively

A headset allows the rider to steer the front wheel effectively and confidently. The handlebar, which is connected to the steerer tube by the stem, turns the fork and the front wheel.

Threadless headset

To determine whether your bike is equipped with a threadless or a threaded headset, look at the stem. If you can see bolts on the side of the part that sits on top of the head tube, it is a threadless headset.

A number of different types of threadless headsets can be installed on modern bikes. These range from the type that has both top and bottom cups, like the traditional headset, to others, such as the headset illustrated here, where the bearing surfaces fit inside the head tube. All the various types of headsets work on the same principle and are taken apart in a similar way.

Occasionally, you need to strip down the headset in order to check it for wear and to clean and lubricate the bearings. If you find any cups or bearing surfaces are worn, you will need to replace the whole headset. This job requires special equipment and is best left to the experts in a good bike shop.

STEP LOCATOR

Parts of a threadless headset

Stem cap

Stem cap bolt

Top bearing cover

Top race

Bottom cup

Toolbox

● Allen key multi-tool ● Degreaser ● Grease

Adjusting and cleaning a threadless headset

1 **Remove the stem cap bolt** from the center of the stem cap with an Allen key. This bolt loads the headset to prevent play in it, rather than securing the stem.

4 **Lower the fork** and lift off the top spacers and either the top cup or bearing cover, depending on the type of threadless headset.

● Clean, degrease, and look at the bottom bearing. If there are no signs of wear, grease the bearing.

● Take the centering wedge out of the head tube. Clean the bearings, bearing surfaces (*inset*), and bearing cover or top cup. Examine for wear, put new grease on the bearings, and reinstall.

2 **Loosen the clamp bolts** on the side of the stem once you have removed the cap bolt. The stem and handlebar assembly are now free. It is the stem clamp bolts that secure the stem to the steerer.

3 **Take hold of the front fork,** then lift the stem and handlebar from the steerer. You can leave these to hang out of the way, supported by the brake and gear cables.

5 **Put the fork back** into the head tube and replace the centering wedge, bearing cover, and spacers.

● Put the handlebar and stem back on top of the steerer.

● Load the headset by tightening the stem cap bolt to a point where the handlebar turns freely, but there is no play in the headset. Secure the stem in place by tightening the clamp bolts.

● Apply the front brake and try to push the bike forward to make sure the headset is not loose.

Threaded headset

Older bikes and children's bikes are equipped with threaded headsets. This type of headset is designed to make it easy to raise and lower the stem whenever you want to change the height of the handlebar and adjust your riding position.

The headset's top cup and the locknut that holds it in place are both screwed onto the steerer. The stem is equipped with a shaft, or quill, that fits inside the steerer. For safety reasons, you should never raise a stem above the limit marked on its quill.

On some very old headsets, the top cup screws down. Its serrated top edge is held in place by a clamp bolt on a similarly serrated lockring assembly. When the clamp bolt is loosened, the top cup screws off.

Remember to disconnect the brakes before you start working on the headset and make sure that you reconnect them when you are finished. Before the stem is replaced into the steerer of the headset, coat the quill with grease (see *pp.38–9*).

STEP LOCATOR

Parts of a threaded headset

Spacer — Locknut

Top race — Top cup

SHIMANO ULTEGRA

Bottom cup

SHIMANO ULTEGRA — Fork crown race

Toolbox

• 6mm Allen key • Grease • Degreaser • 30mm and 32mm headset wrenches • Plastic mallet

Servicing a threaded headset

1 **Undo the Allen bolt** in the stem center and knock it downward with a plastic mallet to free the steerer. The stem is secured into the steerer by an expander bolt, which, as it is tightened, draws a wedge up inside the quill.

• Lift the stem from the steerer.

4 **Degrease all the bearing surfaces** of the top and bottom cups and races. You can access the top bearings by pushing the fork up the head tube and holding it there.

• Inspect the bearing surfaces. If any are damaged, you need a new headset; this is best left to a good bike shop.

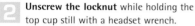
Unscrew the locknut while holding the top cup still with a headset wrench.

- Spread newspaper on the floor to catch loose bearings that may drop out of the top cup.

- Lift off the spacers, then unscrew the top cup upward from the steerer.

Lower the fork to reveal the bearings in the bottom cup. Screwing the top cup upward allows this to happen. Although most headsets have ball bearings held in cages, watch out for loose bearings that may drop out of the bottom cup. Some headsets have roller bearings—treat these as ball bearings in the following steps.

Grease both the top and bottom bearings or set loose bearings in grease inside each cup.

- Completely unscrew the top cup to remove the bearings. Set the bearings individually in the greased cups and screw the top cup back on. Bearings held in cages can be greased in situ provided they are not worn out.

Screw the top cup down onto the top bearings. Replace the spacers and locknut.

- Adjust the top cup so that steering is free.

- Pull the fork to make sure there is no forward movement in the headset.

- Replace the spacer, hold the top cup with a wrench, and tighten the locknut onto it.

- Replace the stem and handlebar.

HANDLEBARS

Most modern bikes are equipped with either straight or drop handlebars. A rider must be able to rely totally on the handlebar, so for safety reasons, a handlebar must be replaced at once if scratches, stress marks, or cracks develop on the surface.

Straight handlebar

Owners of road bikes sometimes want to change the handlebar to a different shape, often to suit the proportions of their body or because of their cycling needs. Some cyclists want to replace a drop handlebar with a straight, or flat, bar. Others may want to replace their existing straight bars with riser bars, or vice versa. Riser bars, which are installed on mountain bikes, are straight in the center, then rise up to become straight where the grips are. They are installed the same way as a straight handlebar.

The steps in this sequence apply to all straight handlebars, whatever the reason for replacing them. However, when replacing a drop handlebar with a straight bar, it will be necessary to swap the brake levers for levers that work with flat or riser bars. Some of these steps will also be useful when installing new grips, brake levers, gear-shift levers, or bar-ends to an existing handlebar.

Parts of a straight handlebar

Plastic plug
Grip
Straight handlebar
Ring clamp
Bar-end
Shifter unit
Brake lever
Clamp bolt

Toolbox
- Half-round file ● Emery paper ● Ruler
- Allen key multi-tool ● Hair spray

STEP LOCATOR

Installing a straight handlebar

1 **Remove any raised pieces of metal** inside the stem clamp with a medium, half-round file (*inset*). Smooth the area with emery paper.

● Place the straight handlebar into the stem clamp and screw in the clamp bolts. Make sure the bar is centered before tightening it fully. If you are installing a riser bar, decide what angle of sweep you want before tightening the bolts.

2 **Secure the ring clamp** of the brake lever to the handlebar. Like road brake levers, off-road levers have a ring clamp that fits over and secures them to the handlebar. Some off-road brake levers have integrated shift levers with only one clamp. However, some are separate and there are two clamps to go over the handlebar.

3 **Spray hair spray** into the handlebar grips to help the grips slide onto the handlebar. When the hair spray dries, the grips will fit tightly to the handlebars.

4 **Slide the grips** onto the handlebar while they are still wet with hair spray.

● Push the grips farther on if you are installing bar-ends to allow for the width of the bar-end clamp.

● Install grip-locks to hold the grips in place and prevent them from twisting while you are riding.

5 **Clamp on the bar-ends.** Line them up parallel with the angle of your stem at first, then adjust their angle to suit your own preference after riding.

● Put a plastic plug in each end of the handlebar to prevent injury in the event of a fall.

Drop handlebar

Road-riding cyclists often install a drop handlebar on their bikes so their bodies can adopt a lower, more aerodynamic posture. However, the handlebar should never be positioned so low that breathing is restricted when holding the bottom of the bar.

Replace a drop handlebar at once if any cracks develop on its surface. The steps in this sequence will show how to replace a drop handlebar and how to install, and therefore how to reposition, brake levers. Cyclists with larger hands and long arms may prefer to mount the levers lower down on the handlebar than the ideal position shown here.

Regularly replace the handlebar tape as shown in Steps 5 and 6, and insert a plug in each end of the handlebar after taping to help prevent injury in a fall.

Brake levers for flat handlebars will not work on drop handlebars, and may not work with all brake types. Check the compatibility of your components before swapping.

STEP LOCATOR

Parts of a drop handlebar

Drop handlebar — Cable groove
Handlebar tape
Brake lever hood — Rubber cover — Brake lever

Toolbox
- Half-round file ● Emery paper
- Allen key multi-tool

Installing a drop handlebar

1 **Use a medium, half-round file** to remove any raised areas of metal inside the part of the stem that clamps the bar in place. These raised areas can bite into the handlebar, eventually causing them to fracture.

● Smooth the filed surface with emery paper.

4 **Secure the levers** of a Campagnolo brake/shift to the handlebar by tightening a bolt on the outside of the hood with an Allen key. Pull the lever hood cover forward to access the bolt. The bolt on Shimano levers is farther down the outer side of the lever hood, so that you need to put your Allen key into a recess under the rubber cover.

Install the new handlebar and tighten up the clamp bolts. Before you secure the bolts, try to line up the flat part of the bottom of the handlebar with a point just below the back brake.

Slide the steel ring of the brake lever over the handlebar. This ring clamps the lever to the handlebar.

- Attach the bolt in the brake lever hood to the screw thread on the ring and tighten.

Pull the cover of the brake lever hood forward and place a short length of tape over each steel ring.

- Wind the tape in one turn from the bottom to the top of the lever hood. When you reach the top of the handlebar, secure the tape with electrical tape.

Start taping at one end of the handlebar.

- Wind upward, covering half of the previous turn with each subsequent turn.

- Keep the tape tight at all times.

Aero bars

If you want to compete in a time trial or a triathlon, or want to achieve a more aerodynamic riding position, you could attach aero bars to the existing handlebar on your bike. Aero bars do not provide the same aerodynamic advantage of the integrated bars used on triathlon- or time-trial-specific bikes, but they do provide a high percentage of it.

Aero bars are simple to install, and they can be removed easily by undoing the fixing-clamp bolts shown in Step 1. Once installed, aero bars must be checked regularly to ensure that the bolts remain tight. Also, test all bolts for tightness with an Allen key after your first ride on them. However, be careful not to overtighten them—sufficient force to stop the bolts from moving is all that is required.

STEP LOCATOR

Parts of an aero bar

Aero bar extension

Fixing clamp

Arm rest

Pad

Toolbox
• Allen key multi-tool • Insulation tape (optional)

Installing aero bars

1 **Assemble the aero bars** from their component parts.

• Position the aero bars on the middle of the handlebar, making sure that each one is placed the same distance from the stem.

• Tighten the clamp bolt on each aero bar with an Allen key, but don't attach the pads yet.

• You can wrap insulation tape around your handlebar before installing the aero bars, to prevent it from being scratched by the clamps.

4 **Attach the pads** to the arm rests. These are usually affixed using sticky-backed velcro.

• Peel off the backing and stick the velcro to the metal arm rest, then attach the pad. You can remove and reposition the pad until you find a comfortable position.

Set the arm rests in the farthest-apart position, using an Allen key on the bolts that secure them in position.

- The arm rests will either fit on the aero bar extensions, or onto the handlebar itself, to the outside of the aero bar extensions.

Your arms should be fairly wide apart when you sit in an aerodynamic tuck position, so that they don't restrict your breathing.

- Get somebody to help you or use a mirror. Your hands should be close together, but your upper arms should be as close to vertical as possible.

- Move the arm rests to achieve the pictured body position by moving the rests in or out, then reattaching them (*inset*).

Adjust the reach of the aero bar extensions until you achieve a riding position where your elbow joint is flexed at an angle of 90 degrees.

- Most aero bar extensions can be moved forward and backward by undoing an Allen-key clamp bolt.

HUBS

There are two types of hubs, open-bearing and cartridge. The cones and bearings of open-bearing hubs must be adjusted to let the hubs spin freely, with little play. The bearings in both types of hubs need regular checking and lubrication.

How they work

The hub allows the wheel to revolve. Quick-release mechanisms or nuts secure the axle into the bike's frame. The axle remains static while the hub body spins around on bearings. Spokes run from the hub's flanges to the rim of the wheel—as the hub spins, so does the rim.

The drivetrain transfers the rider's power from the pedals to the rear wheel, while the front wheel is essentially pushed along by the revolutions of the rear. The gears on a bike are located on the rear hub, either as a hub-gear unit or as multiple cogs in the case of derailleur gears.

The freewheel mechanism, which is also on the rear hub, allows a rider to stop pedaling while the bike is in motion—for example, on a downhill stretch of road. This mechanism is part of the hub in both hub gears and hubs with cassette cogs.

Minimizing friction
Free-spinning hubs are an essential part of an efficient bike. Their bearings must create as little friction as possible, so as not to slow the rider's forward progress.

EXPLODED CARTRIDGE HUB

The axle of a cartridge hub is not threaded, so the bearings are pushed onto each end of the axle and covered by a seal. When the hub is assembled, the bearings sit in the hub body, just to the outside of the flanges, with the axle running through them. Lockrings ensure that everything is held in place.

Axle
Rotates the wheel

Flange
Anchors the spokes to the hub

Seal
Covers the bearings

Hub body
Contains the axle

Cartridge bearings
Support the hub body

Open-bearing front hub
Allows the wheel to revolve smoothly

OPEN-BEARING FRONT HUB ANATOMY

The body on an open-bearing front hub spins on ball bearings that are set within, and at each end of, the hub body. Each set of bearings is held in place by a cone (not visible) that is screwed down on the thread at the end of the axle. A locknut (not visible) locks the cone in place on the same thread. If the hub is held by a quick-release mechanism, the axle is hollow to allow the quick-release skewer to go through it.

Axle
Remains static as the wheel revolves

Hub body
Rotates around the axle

Ball bearings
Support the hub body

Quick-release skewer
Locks the axle in place

Open-bearing hub

Hubs are available in two types—open-bearing or cartridge. The open-bearing hubs require much more maintenance than the cartridge type, since their bearings need regular inspection, cleaning, and regreasing. As a result, the ability to strip down and service an open-bearing hub is a skill that can be used repeatedly.

The following steps will help you remove an axle and a freehub, as well as regrease and retighten the bearings. They can be applied to a Shimano front or rear hub and a Campagnolo front hub. However, leave servicing a Campagnolo rear hub to the experts at a bike shop because it requires specialized tools.

If you are working on a rear hub, you need to remove the cassette by following the steps on pp.80–1 before tackling the steps in this sequence.

STEP LOCATOR

Parts of an open-bearing hub

Locknut Flange   Flange Freehub body
          Hub
Cone   body   Locknut

Spacers   Axle

Non-drive side   Drive side

Toolbox

- 15mm and 16mm cone wrenches (Shimano)
- 13mm and 14mm cone wrenches (Campagnolo)
- Grease • Grease gun (optional)
- Allen key multi-tool • Adjustable wrench
- 8mm or 10mm Allen key

Overhauling an open-bearing hub

1 **Remove the locknut** on the drive side with a wrench while holding the non-drive-side cone with a cone wrench. Some locknuts can be removed with an ordinary wrench, others with an Allen key.

- Keep holding the non-drive-side cone with the cone wrench and remove the drive-side cone with another cone wrench.

4 **Install a new hub body** or the cleaned old one by reversing Step 3.

- Reinsert the axle from the non-drive side. Tighten the drive cone up to the bearings and make sure the axle spins freely with minimal play.

- Lock the cone into position with the locknut. Use the cone wrenches to make sure the non-drive cone is tight against its locknut.

2 **Pull the axle out** from the non-drive side. Be careful not to dislodge the ball bearings.

• Clean the cones and axle and inspect them for damage. Check to see if the axle is bent by rolling it on a flat surface and looking for irregular motion. Replace damaged cones or bent axles immediately.

• Remove the bearings and clean with degreaser. Replace any that have scores or flat spots on their surface. Reinsert and pack with grease (*inset*).

3 **Insert an Allen key** into the 8mm or 10mm Allen bolt located in the center of the freehub. This bolt holds the freehub body onto the axle.

• Turn the key counterclockwise to remove the freehub. You may need a bit of force to loosen this bolt so use an Allen key with a long handle for extra leverage.

5 **Mavic wheels**, as well as some made by other manufacturers, have a simple way of taking up any slack and wear in the bearings.

• Remove the wheel from the bike, and the quick-release skewer from the hub axle.

• The inside ends of the axle are shaped to receive an Allen key. Place an Allen key in each end of the axle and tighten the cones. Tighten only enough to take up any slack—do not overtighten as this can damage the bearings.

WHEELS

Quick-release mechanisms help remove and replace a wheel quicker than ever before. The tires are the component that make contact with the ground. Match the tires on your bike to the prevailing riding conditions and always be ready to replace worn-out tires.

Quick-release wheels

Removing and reattaching a wheel is a straightforward task, but if any of the following steps are overlooked, the wheel may come loose and compromise the rider's safety. The steps are for wheels with quick-release levers that secure them in the drop-outs (the recess in the frame into which the axle fits). For bikes with axle nuts, loosening and tightening with a wrench corresponds to unlocking and locking the quick-release lever.

Levers are labeled "locked" or "closed" on the side facing the cyclist when the wheel is secure, and "unlocked" or "open" when it is not. Make sure levers are locked before each ride, and during a ride if disc brakes are used.

The rim brake needs to be released on the wheel being removed. For V-brakes, unhook the cable from its cradle; for cantilevers, unhook the straddle wire from the left brake arm; for calipers, use the quick-release lever.

STEP LOCATOR

Parts of the quick-release system

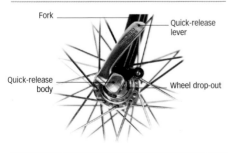

Fork

Quick-release lever

Quick-release body

Wheel drop-out

Toolbox
● Wrenches for wheels with axle nuts

Removing a rear wheel

1 **Release the brake,** shift the chain onto the smallest cog, and pull the quick-release lever away from the bike into the unlocked position. Some quick-release levers are shaped so that they bend toward the frame when in the locked position. This provides a visual check if nothing is printed on the lever.

Removing a front wheel

1 **Release the brake.** Pull the quick-release lever to the unlocked position. If the drop-out has safety lips, the wheel will not come out of the fork at this stage. These safety lips prevent the wheel from falling out in the unlikely event of the lever becoming unlocked while you ride.

● Use your fingers to unscrew the nut on the opposite side of the lever until the quick-release clears the safety lip.

2 **Lift up the bike** to allow the wheel to drop out of the fork.

● Replace the front wheel by reversing Step 1.

● Push the quick-release lever behind the left fork leg to prevent anything from catching it and opening it accidentally.

● Reconnect the brake once the wheel is locked.

2 **Hook the chain** out of the way and onto the peg situated on the inner side of the right seat stay (if there is one).

● Pull the rear derailleur back and then lift up the rear of the bike.

● Give the tire a sharp blow from above with the heel of your hand if the wheel does not drop forward and out of the frame.

3 **Replace the wheel** by introducing the hub axle to the drop-outs.

● Hook the chain onto the smallest cog, then push or pull the wheel backward.

● Line up the tire exactly in the middle of the chainstays as you hold the wheel straight.

● Push the quick-release lever into the locked position to secure the wheel. Reconnect the brake.

Puncture repair

When you are out on a ride, it is much easier to replace a punctured inner tube with an intact tube rather than painstakingly mending the puncture. At home, you can repair the punctured tube with adhesive and a patch. It is still a good idea to carry a repair kit on every ride, because you might be unlucky enough to get a second puncture and be forced to repair the tube outdoors.

The main point to remember about fixing a puncture is not to rush any of the stages. If you patiently give the glue time to dry, closely examine the inside of the tire, and carefully reinstall the tube, then you will be rewarded with a successful repair. If you miss anything or pinch the inner tube, you may get another puncture.

STEP LOCATOR

Parts of a wheel

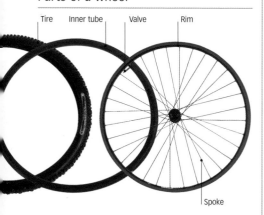

Tire   Inner tube   Valve   Rim

Spoke

Toolbox

● Tire levers ● Crayon ● Sandpaper ● Chalk
● Patch adhesive ● Repair patches

Fixing a punctured inner tube

1 **Take the wheel off** of the bike. Place one tire lever under the tire bead and lift it off the rim. Hook this lever around one of the spokes.

● Insert another lever under the tire near the hooked lever. Push the second lever forward and run it around the whole circumference of the rim to remove one side of the tire.

● Remove the inner tube from the rim.

4 **Take the tire off the wheel,** turn it inside out, and thoroughly check the inner surface.

● Remove anything that is sticking through the tire by pulling it out from the outside of the tire.

2 **Inflate the tube** a little and listen for the sound of escaping air. Locate the hole, mark it with a crayon, and let the air out of the tube.

● Spread a thin layer of adhesive over and around the hole (*inset*). Allow time for it to become tacky.

● Peel the foil from the patch. Press the patch firmly onto the adhesive for over a minute. Make sure the edges are flat.

3 **Use a small piece of sandpaper** to dust some chalk over the patch to prevent excess adhesive from sticking to the inside of the tire.

● Leave the tube for a few minutes to make sure that the adhesive has dried.

5 **Put one side of the tire** all the way back onto the rim. Slightly inflate the tube, insert the valve into the hole in the rim, and work the tube back inside the tire.

● Put the other side of the tire in place by pushing the valve upward, then lifting the section of tire next to the valve over the rim. Work the tire back around the rim.

● Make sure the tire has not pinched the tube underneath it before fully inflating the tube. To do this, squeeze the tire together and look around the whole circumference of the wheel.

Spokes and rims

The steps in this sequence explain how to replace a single broken spoke and also how to true a wheel, a term for straightening the rim of a wheel. However, replacing multiple spokes, replacing spokes in nonstandard wheels, and trueing a wheel that has been buckled by some kind of impact are jobs that are best left to the experts in a good bike repair shop.

It is essential to true the wheel after replacing a broken spoke because the wheel rim is kept straight by the combined pull of all the spokes acting on it. If one spoke breaks, its pull is eliminated and the rim as a whole goes out of line.

A wheel jig is needed to true a wheel properly. This tool holds the wheel securely in place, and its jaws provide a reference point on either side of the rim to help judge how far out of line the wheel is. Bringing it in line is a matter of tightening the new spoke until it reaches the same tension as the old spoke.

STEP LOCATOR

Parts of a spoke

Spoke head

Spoke

Bend

Nipple head | Nipple | Threads | Spoke

Toolbox

- Spoke key • Wheel jig
- Needle-nose pliers

Replacing a spoke and trueing a wheel

1 **Remove the wheel** and take off the tire and inner tube.

- Lift up the rim tape next to the broken spoke and push the spoke upward and out of the rim. If the head of the spoke is broken, measure the broken spoke so you can buy the correct length to replace it. If the break occurred in another place, measure the two pieces to get the right length.

4 **Screw the nipple** onto the spoke. For the first few turns, you can use your fingers.

- Go back to Step 2 and make sure the spoke is laced exactly the same way as the spoke four steps away from it. If it is not laced properly, tensioning the spoke in Steps 5 and 6 could damage the wheel.

2 **Insert the new spoke,** threads first, into the hub flange on the opposite side from its two neighbors.

● Lace the new spoke into the wheel, under and over the neighboring spokes. To do this, look at the spoke four steps away and lace the new spoke exactly the same way.

3 **Push the nipple** of the new spoke through the rim hole from inside the rim and screw it onto the spoke.

● Remove the rim tape to make it easier to fit the nipple onto the new spoke.

● Check the rim tape—if you see any splits, or if it is frayed, replace the tape.

5 **Put the wheel into a wheel jig** and take up the remaining slack on the spoke nipple by tightening it with a spoke key. Make sure that the spoke key is exactly the right size for the nipples on the wheel.

● Stop short of making the spoke as tight as its neighbors at this stage.

6 **Use small, measured turns** of the spoke key to tension the spoke.

● Rotate the wheel so that the nipple of the new spoke is between the jaws of your jig.

● Note how out of line the rim is, then give the nipple a one-quarter tightening turn and check again between the jaws. Repeat and check each quarter-turn until the rim is straight.

ADJUSTING YOUR BRAKES

Trustworthy brakes are a bike's most important component. The braking system needs to be adjusted and serviced carefully and precisely to guarantee a rider's safety in all conditions.

RIM BRAKES

Rim brakes stop a bike by contacting the rim of the wheels. Pads must be checked to ensure that they contact the rim fully and at the same time, and replaced when they are worn. Brake cables must be checked and lubricated regularly.

How they work

The three most common types of rim brake—V-brake, cantilever, and caliper—work in similar ways. A lever pulls a cable, which causes the two brake arms to move toward each other simultaneously. This action brings the two pads into contact with the braking surface of the wheel rim. Springs cause the arms to move back when the lever is released. Cantilever brakes distribute the cable's pull via a straddle wire. The inner cable in a V-brake and caliper pulls one arm, while the outer, in resisting this pull, effectively pushes the other arm.

Braking safely
Rim brakes must be set up properly and maintained to very high standards if they are to work effectively and safely on any surface and in all conditions.

V-BRAKE ANATOMY

The cable of a V-brake is attached to a brake arm by a cable-clamp bolt. When pulled, the cable pulls this arm toward the rim. At the same time, the cable-guide tube, which is an extension of the cable housing, pushes the other arm inward. The two arms pivot around the brake bosses, pushing the brake pads against the braking surface on the rim. Once the cable's pull is released, springs around the pivot bolts push the brake arms apart.

Cable-guide tube
Pushes the brake arm

Brake arm
Pivots inward on a brake boss

Inner cable
Pulls the brake arm

Cable-clamp bolt
Attaches the cable to the brake arm

Brake boss
Allows the brake arm to pivot

Brake pad
Contacts the rim and stops the wheel

Springs
Push brake arms apart

Pivot bolt
Anchors the brake arm to the brake boss

Brake lever
Pulls the cable

Brake arm
Moves the brake pads toward the rim

Brake pad
Slows down the wheel

BRAKE LEVER ANATOMY

When the rider applies the brake lever, it pulls the nipple of the inner cable. As it leaves the lever, the brake cable runs inside a cable housing, which sits in a barrel adjuster. This barrel adjuster allows the brake travel to be fine-tuned.

Nipple
Fixes inner cable to brake lever

Brake lever
Pulls the nipple

Inner cable
Links the brake arm to the brake lever

Barrel adjuster
Adjusts brake travel

Cable housing
Resists the pull on the cable

Drop handlebar brake cable

Brake cables on a drop handlebar need to be changed at regular intervals, although this depends on how much the road bike is used. For a heavily used bike, change the brake cables every two months; for a bike ridden lightly two or three times a week, change the brake cables once a year.

The steps in this sequence are performed on the back brake. Replacing a cable on the front brake follows the same principles, but there are no cable guides to thread through.

Brake levers that fit on a drop handlebar require a brake cable with a pear nipple. Always keep a new cable in the toolbox or workshop as a spare. A rear cable can be cut to fit the front as well. Once the cable has been removed, remember to put a few drops of lubricant on the pivots around which the brake lever moves, and spray some oil into the tube inside the lever hood where the cable is inserted.

STEP LOCATOR

Parts of a brake lever and brake cable

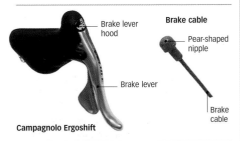

Brake lever hood

Brake cable

Pear-shaped nipple

Brake lever

Brake cable

Campagnolo Ergoshift

Toolbox

- Needle-nose pliers ● Cable cutters
- Allen key multi-tool ● Fine round file

Replacing road bike brake cables

1 **Loosen the cable–clamp bolt** on the brake caliper. Remove the old cable by pulling its nipple from the lever hood with needle-nose pliers.

● Note exactly where the cable fits in the lever hood to allow you to install the new one easily.

● If the old cable has broken, remove the part of the cable that is still clamped to the caliper.

● Carefully unwind the handlebar tape.

4 **Fit each length** of cable housing with a metal ferrule at both ends. When you apply the brake, ferrules prevent the cable housings from being pulled through the cable guides on the frame.

● Make sure that each ferrule is pushed all the way on. Put a little oil on the end of the ferrule to help it slide into place, and wipe off any excess.

2 Insert the new, greased cable into the cradle on the lever in which the nipple sits.

● Thread the cable into the tube in the lever hood. Push it in and watch for it to come out of the back of the lever hood. Now pull it through the lever hood from behind.

● Make sure that the nipple is seated in the brake lever cradle when the cable is all the way through.

3 Cut the new cable housing to length with good-quality cable cutters. Measure the old housing and cut the new one to the same length.

● Always cut between the spirals of the housing.

● Dribble oil into the housing, holding it while the oil runs down to coat the inside.

● Renew cable housings at regular intervals.

5 Thread the cable through the first length of cable housing and the first cable guide.

● Pull the cable all the way through and insert it into the next guide, then the next outer.

● Push the cable housings firmly into the guides to ensure there is no slack when applying the brakes.

● Use a fine round file to file out any tight cable guides. Do not file more than you have to.

6 Pull the cable through the cable-clamp bolt on the caliper until each brake pad is about 2mm from the wheel rim.

● Hold the cable and tighten the clamp bolt. If the brake has a quick-release, make sure it is in the closed position before tightening the clamp bolt.

● Follow Steps 5 and 6 on p.111 to retape the handlebar, with either new or existing tape.

Straight handlebar brake cable

Replacing brake cable inners and housings is a job that should be done fairly often on a mountain bike—about once every 6 to 12 months. They also need to be replaced if they start fraying and become worn. The hybrid bike in this sequence has V-brakes, but some mountain bikes are equipped with cantilever brakes. Installing cables is similar for both.

Brake cables also require regular cleaning and lubrication, especially if the bike has been ridden consistently in wet weather. All brake levers that fit onto a straight or riser handlebar require a cable with a barrel nipple.

Regardless of the manufacturer, the barrel nipple fits into the brake lever in the same way. Remember to use ferrules on both ends of every length of new cable housing. Put a cable crimp on the end of the cable once everything is secure and working properly.

In these steps, the tire is removed from the wheel to show clearly what is happening.

STEP LOCATOR

Parts of a brake lever and a brake cable

Brake lever   Ring clamp   **Brake cable**

Reach adjuster   Nipple

Brake cable

Brake lever   Barrel adjuster

Toolbox

- Needle-nose pliers • Cable cutters
- Allen key multi-tool • Cable pullers (optional)

Replacing V-brake cables on a hybrid bike

1 **Undo the cable–clamp bolt** on the brake. Note where the nipple sits in the cradle that is part of the lever and remove the cable from inside the brake lever by pulling it out with needle-nose pliers.

- Check the cable housings. If they are not worn, you can use them again. Flush them out with degreaser and dribble oil into them.

4 **Attach the cable** to the brake arm by inserting it into the cable guide tube and then pull it through the cable-clamp bolt.

- Keep the cable under tension and make sure each length of cable housing is properly seated in the cable guides.

- Pull the cable to bring the brake pads closer to the rim. Tighten the clamp bolt when the pads are about 2mm from the rim.

2 **Cut new cable housings** to the same length as the housings you removed or measure them on your bike and trim as needed. Buy cable housing either in a roll or in precut lengths with inners in a cable kit. The precut lengths may be too long for your bike, so you may still have to cut to fit.

● Dribble oil into each cable housing and push a metal ferrule onto each end.

3 **Grease the new inner** and thread it into the brake lever. When it shows through the barrel adjuster, pull it from this side of the lever until the nipple is seated in the lever cradle.

● Thread the cable through the lengths of cable housing and seat the cable housings in the cable guides of the frame.

5 **Pull the brake lever** until the brake is fully applied. This ensures that all cable outers are bedded in and all bolts are tight.

● Undo the cable-clamp bolt and repeat Step 4 if the cable slips through the clamp bolt or a ferrule is not seated properly.

6 **Cut off any excess cable** once the cables are bedded in.

● Leave about 1½in (4cm) of free cable after the cable-clamp bolt.

● Put a cable crimp on the end of the cable to prevent it from fraying.

Caliper brake

Maintaining caliper brakes is a question of regularly checking the action of the brake lever. If you have to pull it too far before the brake bites, the brake needs to be adjusted. Check the brake pads for wear and alignment, and make sure they contact the braking surface of the rims simultaneously.

How far the lever has to be pulled before the brake comes on depends on the rider. People with smaller hands may prefer more travel in the lever before the brake bites, because they will pull with more strength the closer the lever is to the handlebar.

Except for their quick-releases, all dual-pivot caliper brakes (such as the Shimano brakes shown here) work in the same way, regardless of the manufacturer. These steps apply to any caliper brake, including those often found on children's bikes.

STEP LOCATOR

Parts of a caliper brake

Travel adjuster, spring, and washer

Caliper arm

Center-fixing bolt

Centering adjusting screw

Brake shoe bolt

Brake pad

Brake shoe

Toolbox
- Full set of Allen keys or Allen key multi-tool
- Needle-nose pliers (optional)

Adjusting a caliper brake

1 **Periodically check for pad wear.** If the pads are wearing down toward half their original depth, they must be replaced.

- Undo the Allen key pad retainer and push out the pad. If the pad and shoe are a complete piece, replace the whole unit, releasing the old pad and installing the new one with a 5mm Allen key.

3 **Pull the brake on** with the brake lever and check to see if both pads simultaneously come in contact with the braking surface on the rim of the wheel.

- Make sure that both sides are working together by turning an adjustment screw on the side of the caliper with an Allen key. This process is called "centering" the brakes.

Using quick-release mechanisms

2 **Adjust the brake pads** so they are directly in line with the braking surface of the rim.

• Release the 5mm Allen bolt on the pad and line the pad up with the braking surface.

• Look for pad wear at this point. Pads that have been set too low will develop a lip and will need to be replaced.

1 **Use a quick-release mechanism** when the adjusted brake pads are so close to the rim that it is impossible to remove the wheel. Campagnolo and Shimano caliper brakes are equipped with different quick-release systems.

• Lift the small lever on the cable-fixing bolt to make Shimano caliper brake pads move away from the rim. After replacing the wheel, lower the lever.

4 **Adjust the brake travel** if you have to pull the brake lever back a long way toward the handlebar before the wheel stops moving.

• Undo the cable-fixing bolt and squeeze the sides of the caliper until the pads nearly touch the rim. The brake cable will then move through the fixing bolt.

• Tighten the bolt and release the caliper.

1 **Press the small button** at the side of the brake lever to move Campagnolo calliper brake pads away from the rim.

• Restore the pads to their original position by pulling the brake lever toward the handlebar until the brakes are on and then push the small button back.

V-brake

V-brakes are fitted to most new mountain bikes because they give good stopping power. Maintaining brake performance is crucial because of the harsh conditions to which mountain bikes are sometimes subjected, so knowing how to adjust the brakes at home and out on the trail is very important.

Pad alignment and brake travel need to be checked and adjusted regularly to keep them working properly. Bear in mind that as soon as you ride off-road you will increase brake pad wear. Even a single ride can render already worn pads useless, so change them before they need it.

Adjustment in the workshop, especially pad alignment, is best performed with the tire removed, since off-road tires are bulky and can get in the way. Wheels must run true before setting up brakes (see pp.122–3).

STEP LOCATOR

Parts of a V-brake

Cradle

V-brake arm

Spacers

Spring clip

Cable-fixing bolt

Pivot bolt

Brake shoe

Brake pad

Toolbox

● Full set of Allen keys or Allen key multi-tool
● Phillips screwdriver ● Cable puller (optional)

Adjusting a V-brake

1 **Make sure the stopper** pin on each brake arm is seated in the same hole on the brake bosses. If it is not, remove the pivot bolt, slide the brake arm off the boss, and put the pin into the correct hole.

● Replace the pivot bolt and retighten it. If you noticed that the brake boss was dry with the arm removed, smear a little grease on it.

4 **Retension the brakes** by hooking the cable back in its cradle.

● Make sure the gap between each brake pad and the rim of the wheel is 1mm.

● Undo the cable-fixing bolt with an Allen key and pull the cable through until the 1mm gap is achieved. Then tighten the cable-fixing bolt.

2 **Press the brake arms together.** If they are not vertical when the pads touch the rim, rearrange the spacers on either side of the pads until they are vertical.

- Release the brakes by unhooking the cable-guide tube from the cradle. Do this when you remove the wheel with correctly adjusted V-brakes.

3 **Undo the brake-pad** fixing bolt, remove the pad and shoe assembly, and switch the spacers around.

- Check the pads. If they are worn, remove the pad-retaining clip, push the old pad out of the shoe, and replace it with a new one.

- Line up the pads so that they hit the rim with their entire braking surface, and are parallel to it. Then tighten the fixing bolts.

5 **Use a Phillips screwdriver** to tighten or loosen the centering screw on each brake arm. The aim is to make both arms move an equal distance before the pad touches the rim when you apply the brake lever.

- The tension on each screw should ideally be even, since there is an equal number of spacers on either side of the brake arm.

6 **Screw out the barrel adjuster** on the brake lever to reduce brake travel and make the brakes feel more responsive.

- Screw the adjuster outward to reduce brake travel and create firmer braking. This technique is quick and easy to perform, and is especially useful for riding in wet conditions, when brake pads can wear down rapidly.

Cantilever brake

Cantilever brakes work with the brake levers that fit dropped handlebars, whereas V-brakes do not. This is why touring and cyclo-cross bikes are fitted with cantilevers. Cantilevers were the predecessors of V-brakes, so they may also be installed on older mountain and hybrid bikes.

Keep cantilever brakes running smoothly by regularly checking the pads for wear and adjusting the pad alignment and brake travel.

The cable of the cantilever brake shown in these steps is clamped to one brake arm and the straddle wire running off it attaches to the other arm. On some older cantilever brakes, the brake cable is attached to a straddle. This hooks the straddle wire that transfers the cable's pull to both brake arms and needs regular adjustment.

STEP LOCATOR

Parts of a cantilever brake

Brake shoe   Brake pad
Cantilever arm   Cable-clamp bolt
Spring clip
Brake pad Allen nut   Spacers

Toolbox

- 5mm Allen key ● Grease gun (optional)
- Grease

Adjusting a cantilever brake

1 **Disconnect the straddle wire** by pushing the cantilever arm to which it is attached toward the wheel with one hand. At the same time, unhook the nipple on the straddle with the other hand.

- Undo the pivot bolts that attach the cantilever arms to the frame bosses.

- Remove the cantilever arms.

1 mm

2 mm

4 **Angle the pads** so that the front of each pad hits the rim before the rear when the brakes are applied—this is called "toe in."

- Loosen the pad-fixing bolt and place an emery board between the rear of the pad and the rim. Apply the brakes and then tighten the bolt. Release the brakes and remove the emery board. Ideally, the front of the pad should be 1mm from the rim and the rear 2mm.

2 **Clean the exposed frame bosses** with a cloth soaked in degreaser, then lubricate with a light grease, not a heavy-duty industrial grease. Use a grease gun if you have one.

● Bolt both arms back onto the bosses, making sure that the stopper pins are inserted into the same hole on each boss.

● Replace the pivot bolts and then tighten them to hold the brake arms to the bosses.

3 **Check the pads.** If one is worn or badly aligned, undo the pad-fixing bolt with an Allen key and remove the pad/shoe assembly.

● Remove the spring clip from the brake shoe and slide out the worn pad. Slide in a new pad and replace the spring clip.

● Return the assembly to the brake arm, line up the pad so that its entire surface contacts the rim, and is parallel with it, then tighten the bolt.

5 **Undo the brake-cable clamp** to achieve the proper spacing from the pad to the rim.

● Pull the cable through the clamp until the front of each brake pad is 1mm from the rim. Tighten the clamp bolt.

● Pull the brake lever to see if both brake arms contact the rim simultaneously. If they do not, screw the centering screws in or out on each arm until they do.

● BMX U-brakes are similar to cantilever brakes, except the straddle wire is held by a straddle clamp. To adjust them, move the pads closer to the rim by undoing the straddle-clamp bolt and pulling the main brake cable through it, then retighten.

HUB-MOUNTED BRAKES

Hub-mounted brakes stop a bike by slowing down the speed of the hub. Regularly check disc brake pads for wear and alignment, replacing them when they are worn. Regularly check and replace the cables on cable discs and hub brakes. Examine the hoses of hydraulic brakes for leaks.

How they work

Hub-mounted brakes are activated by the pull of a lever on a cable, which causes pads to contact a braking surface. Springs push the pads away when the lever is released. In disc brakes, the pads act on discs attached to the hub.

In roller and coaster brakes, the pads act on a braking surface inside the hub. The action of the pads on the surface then slows down the hub and therefore the wheel. In hydraulic brakes, the lever's action pushes fluid through a hose; this fluid pushes the brake pads in the caliper into action. Of all the hub-mounted brakes, hydraulic disc brakes offer a rider the best control over the braking forces that can be applied.

Working in any weather
An advantage of hub brakes over rim brakes is that their performance is largely unaffected by adverse riding conditions.

HYDRAULIC DISC BRAKE ANATOMY

When the rider pulls the brake lever, the hydraulic fluid in the hose pushes on the pistons in the caliper. These pistons in turn cause the brake pad on each side of the disc to contact the disc and slow the rotation of the wheel. When the rider releases the brake lever, the pressure of the fluid in the hose decreases, allowing the springs (not visible) in the caliper to push the brake pads apart.

Hose
Contains fluid

Caliper
Contains pistons and two brake pads

Brake pad
Contacts the disc under pressure from the fluid

Disc
Slows down the hub of the wheel under pressure from the brake pads

Hose
Carries the brake fluid from the lever to the caliper

Brake lever
Compresses the brake fluid

HYDRAULIC BRAKE LEVER

Brake hoses are connected to a reservoir of brake fluid on each brake lever. The fluid fills the hoses all the way to the caliper on the wheel. Pulling the brake lever operates a piston in the reservoir, which pushes the fluid down the hose and, as a result, activates the caliper pistons.

Caliper
Houses the braking mechanism

Disc
Slows down the wheel

Replacing disc brake pads

When brake pads wear down, the brakes will not stop the wheel as quickly. Eventually, the pads become so worn that they have to be replaced. Unevenly worn pads should also be replaced immediately and the caliper may need to be realigned (see p.143). Although replacing pads is broadly the same for all makes and models of disc brakes, there are some differences, mostly in the way the pads are retained within the brake caliper. Some brake pads are kept in position within the caliper by retaining bolts, while others rely on the spring that keeps the two pads apart to fix them in place.

Only use replacement pads recommended by the manufacturer of your brakes, and be very careful how you handle the pads.

STEP LOCATOR

Parts of a disc-brake caliper

Brake hose

Caliper

Rotor

Brake pads (not visible)

Toolbox

- Allen or Torx keys
- Flathead screwdriver

Changing the pads

1 **Remove the wheel from the frame** or forks (see pp.118-19), depending on which brake you are working on.

- Taking care not to touch the disc brake rotor, lower the wheel from the bike by supporting it with both hands on the axle, on each side of the hub.

- If you do touch a rotor you must clean it, or the performance of the brake will be reduced (see pp.142-3).

4 **Place the new pads on either side** of the spring, which is V-shaped when looked at from the side. The tabs of the pads should be at the open end of the V. The narrowest part of the V goes into the caliper first.

- Making sure not to touch the pad surface, hold the pad and spring assembly between the thumb and forefinger, ready to put it in the caliper.

Remove the pad from the caliper. The pads on this model are held in place within the caliper by outward pressure from a spring.

● Before you can push the pads out, you need to pry them apart with a flathead screwdriver.

● If your brakes have a mechanism for taking up pad wear, you need to fully wind it out.

● If your bike has a pad-retaining bolt, remove it with an Allen key.

3 **Once the pads are dislodged,** and all internal pressure is off them, squeeze them together. Use the tabs at the front of the pads to pull them free from the caliper. Sometimes they need a gentle push from behind with a flathead screwdriver.

● If you have to push them, take each pad out separately and make sure that the separating spring comes out, too.

5 **Squeeze the pad/spring assembly** together and push it into the open end of the caliper. Slide the assembly all the way in, listening for the "click" sound that indicates it is seated correctly in the caliper. Let go once you hear the "click."

● The pads should separate when you let go of them. If they don't, remove and reassemble them, then push them in again, repeating Steps 2–5.

6 **Put the wheel back in the frame** or fork, making sure the quick-release lever is locked.

● Bed the pads in by spinning the wheel and pulling the brake lever a number of times. Ride the bike for a short time to test the brakes fully.

● Some brakes have micro-adjusters for fine-tuning their action. Adjust this feature if present on your brakes.

Disc-brake care

Cable disc brakes work well in all conditions. Even so, check the brake cables regularly for signs of fraying and keep them well lubricated. If the brakes do not release quickly when you let go of the brake lever, they need to be lubricated. Check brake travel too, since excessive travel can mean that the brake pads are worn.

When lubricating your bike, make sure that the lubricant does not fall on or touch the brake discs or pads. Do not even touch the disc or pad faces, because the grease from your fingers can easily affect their performance. Always clean the discs with a specialized rotor-cleaning fluid.

Check your disc brake rotors regularly for accuracy and cracks, and clean them after every ride to ensure good brake performance. Replace a cracked or buckled rotor at once.

STEP LOCATOR

Parts of a cable disc brake (front)

Cable housing

Hub

Brake cable

Brake caliper

Rotor-mounting bolts

Brake disc

Toolbox
- Allen or Torx keys • Needle-nose pliers
- Rotor cleaner • Clean cloth

Adjusting cable travel

1 **Loosen the cable–clamp bolt** on the caliper and pull through enough cable, with pliers or a cable-pulling tool, to take up any slack in the cable.

• Tighten the clamp bolt. This will reduce the travel on the brakes and is a necessary adjustment if the brake levers need to be pulled a long way before the brakes work.

Taking care of rotors

1 **Check the rotor for accuracy** by inspecting how it moves through the caliper when the wheel is turned. It should run absolutely straight and true.

• Spin the wheel quickly, but make sure you are holding your bike steady.

2 **Screw out the barrel adjuster** to reduce brake travel. The adjuster is just above where the cable housing sits on the caliper body.

- Loosen the fixing clamp to remove the old cable if a new cable is needed. Insert the new cable into the brake lever (see pp.130–1) and follow Steps 1 and 2 with the new cable.

- Lubricate the new cable before you install it.

3 **Align the calipers** with the discs, using the adjustment bolts. Undo these bolts, align the caliper so that its sides are parallel with the disc, and then tighten.

- Align brakes that are not equipped with this adjustment facility by using spacers to pack out the caliper-fixing bolts.

2 **Remove a cracked or buckled rotor** by unscrewing the bolts holding it to the hub with an Allen or Torx key. Replace it with the specific rotor for your type of brake.

- Place the new rotor over the threaded bolt holes in the hub. Screw in and tighten the bolts.

3 **Clean the rotor** with a specialized rotor-cleaning fluid after removing the wheel.

- Spray a little cleaner on either side of the rotor.

- Use a clean cloth to prevent the cleaner from coating other bike parts but also to ensure the rotor is covered with cleaner. Do not polish with it.

Changing brake fluid

Although hydraulic disc brakes need less maintenance than cable disc brakes, air can occasionally enter a hydraulic system. This will compromise braking, requiring you to pull harder on the lever or to pump the lever several times to fully activate the brake. If this is the case, you will need to bleed the air from the hydraulic system by following these steps.

STEP LOCATOR

Toolbox

- Allen key multi-tool • 10mm wrench
- Length of clear hose

Draining and replacing brake fluid

1 **Remove the wheels** from the bike to reduce the chance of brake fluid falling on the brake discs.

- Place a spacer in the caliper between the brake pads.

- Take off the brake fluid reservoir cover on the brake lever with an Allen key. Be careful not to let any of the brake fluid touch your hands.

4 **Angle the bike** so that the reservoir is level, open the bleed nipple, and fill the reservoir with brake fluid. Pour with a smooth, constant stream to minimize air bubbles.

- Squeeze the brake lever all the way to the handlebar and hold it. Close the bleed nipple.

- Never mix brake fluids. Mineral oil or DOT 4 fluids cannot be interchanged.

5 **Repeat Step 4,** filling up the reservoir until there are no more air bubbles flowing through the clear tube when you squeeze the brake lever. You will probably have to repeat this step four or five times before the bubbles in the tube completely disappear.

- Close the bleed nipple once the tube is bubble-free and the reservoir is full.

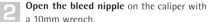
Open the bleed nipple on the caliper with a 10mm wrench.

● Slide one end of a short length of clear tube onto the bleed nipple.

● Put the other end of the tube into a plastic container that is big enough to hold the old brake fluid.

Pull the brake lever all the way back to the handlebar to remove some brake fluid.

● Tighten the bleed nipple.

● Make sure that all tools are at hand, since the next steps require you to be organized.

● Cover the surface below where you are working since brake fluids can be corrosive. Use disposable mechanic's gloves to protect your hands.

Replace the cover of the brake fluid reservoir but be careful not to displace any brake fluid.

● Reattach your wheels and pump the brake lever a few times to center the brake pads.

● Go for a flat test ride. If your brakes are not performing as they should, there may still be air in the system. Repeat Step 4 and make sure that everything is tight.

Roller-brake cable

All brake cables wear out, no matter how much time is spent maintaining them. Cables for roller brakes—sometimes called drum brakes—are no different. If the bike is equipped with roller brakes, the steps in this sequence show how to replace a cable when it is frayed or worn out. However, lubricating the brakes and replacing the internal parts are occasional jobs that are best left to the experts at a good bike shop.

If the rear inner tube is punctured, or it is necessary to take off the back tire to replace it, you need to know how to disconnect the rear brake in order to remove the back wheel. At the same time, you should know how to reconnect and adjust the brake after replacing the wheel. Once this is a familiar routine, it will also be possible to adjust the roller brakes for brake pad wear from time to time.

STEP LOCATOR

5

1 2 3 4 6

Parts of a roller brake

Brake body

Wheel axle nut

Brake arm

Cable-clamp bolt

Barrel adjuster | Cable guide | Cable

Toolbox

- Wrenches
- Needle-nose pliers

Replacing a roller-brake cable

1 **Push the brake-arm cradle** toward the front of the bike. This removes the tension from the cable so that you can unhook the cable-clamp bolt from the cradle and remove the old cable.

- Screw the barrel adjuster on the brake arm in or out to about half of its extent.

- Remove the wheel at this point if you need to replace the tire or inner tube.

4 **Tighten the cable-clamp bolt** while squeezing the cable slightly, as your helper keeps up the forward pull on the brake-arm cradle.

Thread the greased cable through the brake lever, then through the housing.

- Dribble a little oil into the housing.

- Make sure the housing is firmly located in the lever, then thread the cable through the barrel adjuster and seat the housing firmly into it.

- Thread the cable through the cable-clamp bolt.

Pull the cable backward with the needle-nose pliers while you push the brake-arm cradle forward and hook the clamp bolt into it.

- Bend the cable slightly behind the clamp bolt and ask someone to push the brake-arm cradle forward. Use your free hand to tighten up the bolt so the cable is nipped in place.

Pull the brake lever hard repeatedly (ten times) to bed in the brakes. The brakes may be a little tight, as if they are being applied gently even when there is no pressure on the lever.

- Keep about ⅜in (15mm) of play in the brake lever before the brakes begin to bite.

Screw in the barrel adjuster a few turns until you achieve the ⅜in (15mm) of play in the brake lever.

- Pull in the lever after each turn in the adjuster to check when the brakes begin to bite.

TUNING YOUR SUSPENSION

Suspension technology has revolutionized off-road riding. Accurate adjustment of the front fork and the rear shock allows uneven terrain to be tackled safely and confidently.

SUSPENSION FORKS

A suspension fork softens the blow of a bump on the road or trail. The fork must be checked for wear and lubricated regularly. The oil and springs should be changed either when they become worn or to alter the characteristics of the fork.

How they work

The suspension fork on the front wheel absorbs the energy of a bump and prevents the force from reaching the rider. The fork's main spring, which can be trapped air or a metal coil, is compressed as the sliders move up the stanchions. Compression ends when the spring has absorbed the shock of the bump. At this point, the spring pushes the sliders back and the fork rebounds. Damping controls the speed of compression and rebound, usually by absorbing some of the energy of the bump with an air or oil damping mechanism. This creates friction, which slows down the fork's movements.

Reacting to bumps
Damping should prevent the fork from reaching the limits of its travel, but the fork should still be reactive enough to cope with every bump.

FRONT FORK COMPRESSION

Bunnyhopping provides a graphic demonstration of compression and rebound. As the rider picks up the front of the bike to clear the log, the fork rebounds because his weight has been taken off the spring. On landing, the fork compresses as the spring absorbs the shock of the bike and rider landing.

Rebound

Pulling the handlebar upward *and moving the body backward lifts the front wheel so the front fork rebounds.*

Compression

Landing on the ground *returns the rider's weight to the bike's frame and compresses the front fork.*

AIR/OIL FORK

When a bump pushes up the sliders on this fork, a piston moves up the left stanchion, compressing the air. Once the bump has been absorbed, the air pushes the piston back and the fork rebounds. The damping mechanism in the right stanchion, which is full of oil, also moves up and down with the bump, controlling the speed of compression and rebound.

Fork crown
Turns the fork

Brake arch
Connects the two sliders

Seal
Keeps dirt out of fork's interior

Left stanchion
Contains the spring mechanism and piston

Right stanchion
Contains the damping mechanism

Air chamber
Contains air

Oil chamber
Contains oil

Damping mechanism
Moves up and down with slider

Piston
Moves up and down in response to bumps

Slider
Moves up and down on the stanchion

Shaft bolt
Fastens shaft to slider

Front suspension

A suspension fork works best if it has been set up to accommodate the rider's weight. When you sit on your bike, the amount the fork depresses as the slider moves down the stanchion is called the sag. As you ride, sag allows the fork to extend into the hollows in the ground, providing a smooth ride. To set the amount of sag, you can increase or decrease the amount of preload in the fork.

Damping controls the speed at which a fork works. To find out if a fork is working too fast, lean on the handlebar, then quickly lift up the front of the bike. If the suspension fork bangs back to its limit, its action is too quick and its rebound damping needs to be increased. Adjust the damping still further after a few rides. The best setup will allow the fork to absorb a hit and rebound quickly enough to be ready for the next.

STEP LOCATOR

Parts of a suspension fork

Steerer
Air valve
Crown
Stanchion
Fork brace
Brake boss
Slider
Drop-out

Toolbox

● Shock pump ● Cable tie
● Tape measure

Setting sag

1 **Put a cable tie** around the stanchion of the unloaded fork and next to the top of the slider. Ideally, the sag should be about 25 percent of its available travel, though cross-country riders often prefer less and downhillers more.

3 **Get off the bike** and carefully measure the distance between the cable tie and the top of the slider.

● Express this measurement as a proportion of the fork's available travel. If the distance is 1in (25mm) on a 3¹/₅in (80mm) fork, the proportion is 31 percent. Check the owner's manual to find out the available travel of your bike.

Fine-tuning the fork

2 **Sit on the bike,** wearing your normal cycling clothes.

● Place both feet on the pedals. Either ask someone to hold you upright on the bike, or lean your elbow against a wall. The slider will travel up the stanchion, pushing the cable tie with it.

1 **Fine-tune the damping** on some forks with an adjuster at the bottom of one of the fork blades. The two air chambers in this fork allow further refinements to damping.

● Pump air into the bottom chamber with a shock pump to change the spring characteristics.

● Change the size of a valve on the air piston to control air flow between chambers. This flow is called air-damping.

4 **Increase the air** in the chamber with a shock pump if the proportion of available travel is greater than 25 percent.

● Increase the spring preload with a coil/oil system (there is usually a dial at the top of the fork blade) or install stronger springs.

● Release air, reduce the preload, or install lighter springs if the proportion is less than 25 percent.

1 **Make damping adjustments** on some types of fork while riding the bike. The controls for these on-the-fly adjusters are usually marked "faster" and "slower" to indicate which direction to turn them in. It is also possible to lock out some forks. This means that you can stop their action if you are riding over a very smooth surface and do not need suspension.

Coil/oil fork

If the sag has been set up correctly (see pp.152–3) but the coil/oil fork keeps bottoming out—the fork reaches the full extent of its travel but the spring cannot compress any more—it will be necessary to install heavier-duty springs. Conversely, if the fork only reacts to the bigger lumps and bumps, lighter springs should be installed.

The method of changing springs is similar in most coil/oil forks, but check the manufacturer's manual to find the features of the fork on the bike in question. It may not be necessary to remove the fork blade from the fork crown; or a spring in both blades of the fork may need to be replaced; or one blade may contain the spring, while the other contains the damping mechanism.

STEP LOCATOR

1 2 3 4 5

Parts of a coil/oil fork

Steerer
Fork crown
Top cap
Fork crown bolts
Stanchion
Fork brace
Brake boss
Slider
Drop-out

Toolbox

● Wrench ● Allen key multi-tool
● Flathead screwdriver

Setting up a coil/oil fork

1 **Remove the circle** clip from around the rebound adjuster of the fork by prying it off with a flathead screwdriver. Be very careful. Do not dig your screwdriver too far under the circle clip, but put it far enough under so that it does not slip. Keep your fingers away from the screwdriver to avoid injuring yourself if it slips.

4 **Drop the new spring** into the fork blade. Make sure that it sits correctly in the fork blade, then replace the top cap.

● Screw the top cap in with your fingers, then tighten it with a wrench.

2 **Undo the retaining bolts** in the fork crown so that you can drop the blades out. There are usually four retaining bolts. Some fork crowns do not have them, in which case undo a cap bolt at the top of the fork blade to remove the springs.

3 **Start to remove the top cap** of the fork blade with a wrench on the wrench flats, then unscrew the cap the rest of the way out with your fingers.

● Note how the spring is sitting in the fork blade, then lift the spring out.

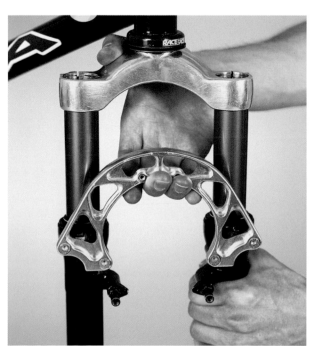

5 **Put the fork blades** back in the fork crown and secure the retaining bolts.

● Follow the manufacturer's torque settings when replacing the retaining bolts.

● Reset the sag of your forks (see pp.152–3).

Air/oil fork

Air/oil suspension forks usually have short travel and are popular with cross-country riders. Their spring medium is air, which makes them very light, and their mechanism is damped by oil.

Sometimes they have a negative spring working in the opposite direction of the main air spring. This helps to overcome the stiction (the static friction between two adjacent but motionless objects) which is inherent in air/oil suspension forks and is caused by their very tight seals.

Changing the oil is necessary from time to time, as dirt in the system starts to cause excessive wear. If you have increased the damping on your fork and its action is still too fast, replacing the oil with a heavier one will slow it down. In the same way, lighter oil can help speed it up.

STEP LOCATOR

Parts of an air/oil suspension fork

Steerer
Fork crown
Stanchion
Air valve
Fork brace
Brake boss
Slider
Drop-out

Toolbox

● Wrench ● Shock pump

Changing the oil

1 **Remove the cap** from the top of the stanchion without the Schrader air valve. This is the same kind of valve that is used on car tires. You can carry out the following sequence of steps with the fork still in the bike, although it is easier if someone helps you.

3 **Make sure that you hold** the fork blades absolutely vertical.

● Place a bowl under the fork to catch any spills. Carefully pour new oil into the stanchion until it is full and then replace the cap.

● Use a calibrated pouring vessel to ensure that you accurately measure the amount of oil, if the fork manufacturer specifies.

2 **Pour the old oil out** of the stanchion and into a plastic cup. This air/oil fork has an open-bath damping system, in which the damping rod moves up and down in an open oil bath. The oil also lubricates the rest of the suspension system.

4 **Put the cap back** on top of the oil stanchion and tighten it.

● Set the sag again (see pp.152–3), pumping air in or letting it out to obtain the ideal sag.

● Tighten the Schrader valve if, after setting up the sag correctly, your fork works well at first, then starts to bottom out (the valve may be leaking). Use an automotive valve key.

5 **Pump air in** or let air out of a fork with negative air springs after you have replaced the oil with one of a different viscosity.

● Adjust the damping of the fork so that it works at the speed you require, then fine-tune its action with the negative spring.

● Pump air in to make the fork more active over small bumps. Let air out to make it less responsive.

Lefty suspension

A Lefty houses its suspension and damping systems in a single leg, removing the need for the two legs of a traditional suspension fork. This prevents mud from clogging the front wheel—a useful thing to have on an off-road bike—and is lighter.

Removing and reattaching the front wheel of a Lefty, cleaning the air filters, and cleaning and lubricating the telescopic leg are essential maintenance tasks. Further maintenance is best left to qualified technicians. The protective rubber boot should be checked for splits, and the system assessed to ensure it is functioning smoothly. Consult a technician if it is not.

STEP LOCATOR

3 4 5 6

1 2

Parts of a Lefty suspension unit

- Filter cover
- Rubber boot
- Upper ring-clamps
- Lower ring-clamp
- Front brake-caliper
- Wheel mounting bolt
- Schrader valve

Toolbox

- Allen key multi-tool • Insulator tape • Rag and sponge for cleaning • Grease • Shock pump

Cleaning and greasing a Lefty

1 **Undo the two Allen bolts** that hold the front disc-brake caliper onto its mount.

- Carefully lift the caliper over the disc rotor and wrap its hose around the handlebar to keep it safely out of the way.

4 **Wash the filter** with soapy water and a sponge or cloth. Rinse it gently and pat it dry, then spray it with a little oil.

- Remove the tape covering the air holes, then carefully place the foam filter back under its rubber cover. Undo the bottom ring-clamp and slide the boot back up to the filter cover, then fold its top lip over the bottom edge of the cover. Secure both in place with the two ring-clamps.

2 **Undo the Allen bolt** in the center of the hub while supporting the wheel in your other hand.

- Once the bolt is undone, carefully lift the wheel off the axle.

- To replace the wheel, carefully lift it onto the axle until you feel the bolt engage. Then tighten it with the Allen key and reverse Step 1 to reinstall the front caliper.

3 **Detach the two ring-clamps** at the top of the rubber boot by loosening the Allen bolts.

- Disengage the lower, longer section of the boot from the smaller top section, then slide the lower section down and secure it with the lower clamp.

- The top section of the boot is the filter cover. Slide it up and pry out the foam filter. This reveals two air holes, one on the front (*inset*) and one on the back of the leg—cover them with tape.

5 **Release the air** from the Lefty by depressing the Schrader valve located at the bottom of the leg (*inset*).

- Undo the ring-clamp at the bottom of the boot, then lift the boot. Wipe all the old grease from the leg with a dry cloth.

6 **Apply new grease**, either with a grease gun or brush. Spread it out as evenly as possible.

- Slide the boot back down the fork leg and reattach it with the ring-clamp.

- Screw your shock pump onto the Schrader valve and reinflate the fork to the personal settings as directed in the Lefty manual (*inset*).

Taking care of suspension forks

Suspension forks soak up a lot of abuse because that is what they are designed to do. Although manufacturers do whatever they can to protect the inner workings, there are still some things you need to do to take care of your forks.

Chief among them is cleaning. If you do not clean your forks regularly, dirt will wear down the seals at the top of the sliders and allow water to get into the inner workings and damage them. Worn seals will also allow oil to leak out, which affects the fork's performance.

Cleaning also gives you the opportunity to examine the forks for cracks and defects. You can also look for telltale signs of seal wear, such as the absence of a dirt ring on the stanchions after a ride—you should see this ring after every ride.

Another one of your regular jobs is to check the fork's settings. You can set the speed at which some forks work, along with other features. You need to make sure these settings have not been reset after a tough ride or after cleaning.

Do not use pressure hoses to clean suspension forks, since they can force water into the inner workings. You need to use a much gentler method to clean this part of your bike.

STEP LOCATOR

1 2 3 4 5 6

Toolbox

- Stiff-bristled brushes • Sponge • Oil
- Degreaser

Cleaning suspension forks

1 **Remove mud and dirt** with a dry, stiff-bristled brush. Remove the front wheel if there is a lot of mud on the fork, since it will make the job easier.

- Start at the top of the fork and brush downward. Make sure not to scrub too hard around the fork seals.

- Use smaller brushes to get into hard-to-reach places on the fork.

4 **Apply light, Teflon-based lubricant** to the seals at the top of the sliders to keep them supple and help maintain their integrity.

- Apply the oil sparingly but make sure you spread it all around the circumference of both seals.

- Be careful not to spill oil on the tires of your bike. If you do spill any, wash it off immediately with hot, soapy water.

2 **Spray degreaser** all over the fork, especially on the stanchions, to remove the old oil and dirt—a mix that could corrode the seals on your fork.

● Again, start spraying degreaser from the top of the fork and work downward.

3 **Wipe the fork clean** with a clean sponge soaked in warm water. Wrap the sponge around the fork to ensure it gets completely rinsed. Start from the top and work down.

● Remove the wheel so you can clean the lower part of the fork thoroughly.

● Examine the fork for cracks and defects while you perform this step.

5 **Pump the fork** up and down by pushing on the handlebars so that the seals become well coated.

● This is a good time to check for cracks on your handlebars and stem.

● Do not be tempted to alter the settings of the fork if it is hard to push. What matters is the way the fork feels when you ride.

6 **Check the settings dials** on your fork. Cleaning, especially when you use a stiff-bristled brush, can move the dials. Make sure they are set where you want them for riding.

● Check the cable outers or hoses for wear over the crown of the fork.

● As a final step, turn your bike upside down for five minutes to help redistribute the oil inside the fork.

REAR SUSPENSION

The rear suspension absorbs the shock caused by a bump in the ground or rough terrain. A shock absorber must be kept clean and lubricated, and the bushings and frame mounts checked regularly for damage and wear.

How it works

The shock absorber of the rear suspension mirrors the specifications of the front fork in order to increase the rider's control of the bike. The rear triangle of the frame, which connects the rear wheel to the shock absorber, can move independently of the rest of the frame on bikes that are equipped with rear suspension.

Shock absorbers—or shocks, as they are also known—consist of a spring medium, either a coil or trapped air, and a shaft. The shaft is usually connected to a damping mechanism, which contains oil and controls the speed of the shock absorber's action.

Adjusting the shock
The shock absorber of the rear suspension can be adjusted to suit different kinds of terrain and gradients.

COMPRESSION OF THE SHOCK ABSORBER

When the back wheel hits a bump on the road or trail, the rear triangle moves up on its pivots, compressing the spring, which absorbs the shock.

As the spring pushes back on the rear triangle of the frame, the shock rebounds, pushing the rear wheel back ready for the next bump.

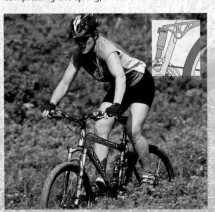

When riding over smooth ground, *the rear shock absorber is in a neutral position.*

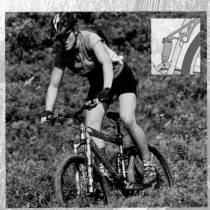

When riding over rough ground, *the rear shock is in a compressed position to absorb bumps.*

AIR/OIL SHOCK ABSORBER ANATOMY

In an air/oil shock absorber, the spring mechanism is compressed air that is sealed inside an air sleeve. The damping mechanism in the shock body contains oil. When the bike hits a bump, the shock body travels up inside the air sleeve and compresses the trapped air. Once this air spring has absorbed the energy of the bump, the shock absorber begins to rebound and return to its original position. The shaft, which runs from the top of the air sleeve into the shock body, is connected to the damping device. Oil flowing through holes in the device slows the action of the shock absorber during compression and rebound as the shock body travels up and down.

Bushing
Attaches shock to frame

Air valve
Controls air pressure in the sleeve

Rebound adjuster
Changes speed of rebound

Shaft
Runs into shock body

Air sleeve
Contains compressed air

Shock body
Contains the damping device

Rear shock
Absorbs the force of a bump

Rear triangle
Transmits the force of a bump to the rear shock

Rear wheel
Moves up and down in response to bumps

Rear suspension

A good-quality full-suspension bike should be designed with a rear shock absorber that complements and works with the suspension fork in the front. Air/oil forks are normally accompanied by an air/oil shock, and coil/oil systems are usually paired together as well.

The first step in setting up a rear shock is to adjust its sag. Take into account the rider's weight, as with suspension forks (*see pp.152–3*), and then fine-tune its action by using damping and the shock's other functions after several rides on the bike.

One simple test to see if a rear shock is working in tune with the front fork is to press down on the middle of the bike, while looking at how the fork and shock react. For general riding, each should depress about the same amount.

Add the frame mounts, to which a shock is attached, to the routine safety checks (*see pp.40–1*). Check the bushings that allow the shock to pivot—consult the manufacturer's guide for instructions.

STEP LOCATOR

1 2 3 4 5

Parts of a rear suspension unit

Pro-pedal adjuster

Shock body

Air sleeve   Air valve   Rebound adjuster

Toolbox

● Tape measure ● Shock pump

Adjusting the sag

1 **Measure the center-to-center** distance between the shock-mounting bolts, with the bike unloaded.

● Familiarize yourself with the valves and various controls of your shock before going further.

3 **To achieve the proportion of sag** that your riding style requires, let air out or pump it in as needed, then take the second measurement again.

● If your bike has a coil/oil shock, increase or decrease the preload to achieve the measurement you want. The recommended range is only a guide.

2 **Sit on the bike** and ask someone to measure this distance again.

● Take both measurements and calculate the second as a percentage of the first. This will reveal the proportion of the shock's overall travel that is used as "sag." For general riding, the figure should be from a quarter to a third.

● Cross-country racers tend to want stiffer shocks, so they sometimes go for a quarter or less.

● Downhill racers like their shocks to move a lot more. Their bikes often feel spongy to ride on flat ground, but are very active when descending.

4 **Fine-tune the damping speed** of your shock with the rebound adjuster—if your bike has one.

● Turn the adjuster on an air/oil shock absorber but follow the instructions on the shock to find out which way to turn.

● Do not set it too fast because this can upset the handling of the bike.

5 **Some shocks have additional** features. The pro-pedal system on this one allows you to control pedal-induced movement of the shock.

● Familiarize yourself with your shock's features by reading the instruction manual.

● Ride your bike across different terrains and see what happens when you vary the settings. Knowing all about your bike and the way you ride will help you get the best out of any trail situation.

Taking care of rear suspension

Rear suspension comes in many forms, but most designs have a rear triangle that pivots on the main frame of the bike, its movement controlled by a shock absorber situated between the rear triangle and the main frame. This allows the rear wheel to move up and down, absorbing shocks while remaining in contact with the ground.

The pivots are mounted on bearings or bushings for smooth movement. Occasionally these components require lubrication, and will eventually wear out. Check the Servicing timetable (see pp.42–3) for when to lubricate. To test for wear, you will need to inspect the bearings and check for play at the pivots from time to time.

STEP LOCATOR

Parts of bushings and bearings

Bearing cover

Small bushing | Large bushing | Small bearing | Large bearing

Toolbox

- Allen key multi-tool • Flathead screwdriver
- Spray degreaser, grease • Rubber mallet or metal-headed hammer • Drift to install bearings

Servicing bearings and bushings

1 **To expose the pivot bearing,** you may need to remove any linkage arms.

- In this case, the linkage arm is attached to the bearing on which it pivots by an Allen bolt. Remove the pivot-bolt with an Allen key, then unhook the linkage.

- Linkages are often bolted together while under load, so you may need someone to help you loosen it by applying counterpressure.

4 **Thoroughly clean** the inside of the bearing seat—the hole where the bearing sits.

- Move the new bearing into place and place the drift squarely on top of it.

2 Use a flathead screwdriver to carefully lift the cover from the bearing (*inset*). This reveals the ball bearings inside.

- Flush out any old dirt and lube with a spray degreaser, then apply new grease to the ball bearings with a grease gun or brush. Apply the grease sparingly but evenly.

- Replace the bearing cover, making sure it is seated firmly in place, then reverse Step 1 to replace any linkage arms.

3 To replace a worn bearing, first detach any linkage arms by undoing the Allen pivot-bolt.

- With the arm and bolt removed, place a drift firmly and flush onto the bearing (*inset*).

- Sharply but carefully tap the drift with a rubber mallet—the bearing should emerge from the other side of the linkage. If the bearing doesn't move, you may need to use a metal-headed hammer to better concentrate the force.

5 Use your mallet to administer sharp but carefully aimed blows, square on the head of the drift.

- As with removing the old bearing, be patient—bearings must be a tight fit. Once the bearing is home, replace the pivot bolt and linkage. Again, you may require help to apply counterpressure.

6 Lubricate any pivot bushings, which are sometimes used on full-suspension bikes.

- These are maintained by occasionally applying thin oil where the two faces contact.

- Like bearings, bushings can also be replaced when worn out. Remove any linkage arms to expose the old bushing, then pry it out with a flathead screwdriver. Clean the bushing seat and press in the new one.

Glossary

Terms in *italics* within an entry are defined under their own headings within the glossary.

ALLEN BOLT A threaded bolt with a hexagonal depression in the center of its head.

ALLEN KEY Hexagonal-shaped tool that fits *Allen bolts.*

BEARING A mechanism that usually consists of a number of ball bearings and circular channels, or races. It allows two metal surfaces to move freely while in contact.

BLOCK Cogs attached to a *freewheel.*

BOSS Threaded metal fixture on a bicycle frame to which an item such as a bottle cage or a pannier rack is attached.

BOTTOM BRACKET Rotating unit that connects the *cranks* on either side of the bottom bracket shell to each other.

BOTTOM OUT A term that describes the point when a *suspension* fork or shock absorber reaches the limit of its *travel.*

BRAKE–LEVER HOOD The body in which the brake lever sits, connecting it to the handlebar.

BRAKE TRAVEL The distance a brake lever moves before the brake pads engage the braking surface on the rim or hub of a wheel.

CABLE END CAP A small, soft-metal cylinder that is closed at one end and fits over the cut ends of a cable to prevent fraying.

CASSETTE *Cogs* that fit on the *freewheel.*

CHAINRING A toothed ring attached to the *cranks,* which drives the chain and, in turn, the *cogs* and the rear wheel of a bicycle.

CHAINSTAY The frame tube joining the *bottom bracket* shell and rear *drop-out.*

CLEAT A plastic or metal plate that attaches to the sole of a cycling shoe and engages into a *clipless pedal* to hold the foot on the pedal.

CLIPLESS PEDAL A pedal with a mechanism to engage the *cleat* on the sole of a cycling shoe and hold it securely in place. Called clipless because they replaced pedals that had toe clips and straps.

COG A toothed ring that is turned by the chain. Combined with other cogs, it forms a *cassette* or *block.*

COMPRESSION The action of a *suspension* system when it absorbs an impact from the terrain. The term refers to the compression of the spring.

CRANK The lever that joins the pedals to the *chainrings* and transfers energy from the rider's legs to the *drivetrain.*

CRANKSET The assembly of *chainrings* and *cranks.*

DAMPING The process that absorbs the energy of an impact transmitted through a *suspension* system. It controls the speed at which any form of suspension responds to uneven terrain.

DERAILLEUR Device that pushes the chain onto a larger or smaller *chainring* or *cog.* See also *Derailleur gears.*

DERAILLEUR GEARS A system that shifts the chain between *cogs* on the rear wheel (rear derailleur) and between *chainrings* attached to *cranks* (front derailleur); it allows multiple gearing on bikes. See also *Derailleur.*

DOWN TUBE The frame tube that joins the *bottom-bracket* shell to the *head tube.*

DRIVETRAIN The assembly of pedals, *crankset,* chain, and *cogs* that drives the bike forward by transforming leg power into wheel rotation. See also *Transmission.*

DROP-OUT A slotted plate at the end of the fork legs and stays, into which the axle of a wheel is attached.

EXPANDER BOLT A bolt that draws up a truncated cone or triangle of metal inside a metal tube in order to wedge the tube in place. Commonly found inside the stem of a threaded *headset.*

FREEHUB A mechanism, which is part of the hub, that allows the rear wheel to rotate while the pedals remain stationary.

FREEWHEEL A mechanism that does the same job as a *freehub* but can be screwed on or off the hub.

GEAR An expression of the *chainring* and *cog* combination, linked by the chain, that propels the bike.

GEAR SATELLITE A disc on a hub gear that rotates when the gear cable is shifted, moving the cogs within the hub in order to change gears.

GEAR-SHIFTER The control mechanism, usually on the handlebar, used to initiate gear-shifts.

GPS Global Positioning System, a satellite-based navigational network used in cycling for navigation and to record speed and other ride data, via a handlebar-mounted device.

GRUB SCREW A headless, threaded bolt with a single diameter throughout its length.

HEADSET The *bearing* unit that attaches the forks to a frame and allows them to turn. There are two varieties: threaded and threadless.

HEAD TUBE The frame tube through which the *steerer tube* runs.

HEXAGONAL BOLT OR NUT A threaded bolt with a hexagonal-shaped head, or a hexagonal-shaped nut that fits onto a threaded bolt.

HYDRAULIC A mechanical system that uses compressed fluid to move an object.

LOCKRING/LOCKNUT A ring or nut used to tighten onto a threaded object and lock it in place.

NEGATIVE SPRING A device that works against the main spring in a *suspension* system. In compression, for example, a negative spring works to extend the fork, helping to overcome the effects of *stiction*.

NIPPLE The piece of metal attached to the end of a cable that secures the cable in the control lever.

PLAY A term to describe any looseness in mechanical parts.

QUICK-RELEASE MECHANISM A lever connected to a skewer that locks or releases a component from the frame.

REBOUND A term to describe the action of a *suspension* system after it absorbs an impact from the terrain. It refers to the extension of the system's spring.

SEAT POST A hollow tube that holds the saddle and is inserted into the *seat tube*.

SEAT STAY The frame tube joining the *bottom bracket* shell and rear *drop-out*.

SEAT TUBE The frame tube that holds the *seat post*.

SIDEWALL Part of the tire between the *tread* and rim.

SPROCKET A circular metal object with teeth. Both *cogs* and *chainrings* are examples of sprockets.

STEERER TUBE The tube that connects the fork to the *stem* and handlebar.

STEM The component that connects the handlebar to the *steerer tube*.

STICTION A term that combines the words static and friction. It describes the tension between moving and static parts at rest, such as the seals and stanchions in a *suspension* fork.

STOPPER PIN The end of a cantilever or V-brake return spring that fits into a locating hole on the bike's brake mounting *bosses*.

SUSPENSION An air/oil or a coil/oil system that absorbs the bumps from a trail or road. The system is either integrated into the fork or connected to the rear wheel via a linkage.

THREADS The spiral grooves cut into metal that allow separate parts to be screwed or bolted together.

TOP TUBE The frame tube that joins the *seat tube* to the *head tube*.

TRANSMISSION A bike's transmission is made up of those parts that transfer the rider's energy into forward motion—the pedals, chain, *crankset*, and *cogs*. See also *Drivetrain*.

TRAVEL A term that refers to the total distance a component moves in carrying out its purpose. For example, travel in a *suspension* fork is the total distance the fork has available to move in order to absorb a shock.

TREAD The central part of a tire that makes contact with the ground.

VISCOSITY A rating system for oils, which also refers to the weight. A light oil has low viscosity and moves quicker than a heavy oil through a given *damping* mechanism. This results in a faster-acting *suspension* system or reduced damping.

WHEEL JIG A stand that holds a wheel so that its rim runs between two jaws. Used in truing a wheel after replacing a broken spoke.

Index

Acknowledgments

Author's acknowledgments

Pip Morgan and Richard Gilbert for their patient and diplomatic editorial work.

Ted Kinsey for designing everything so that the writing makes sense.

Dave Marsh of the Universal Cycle Centre for technical advice regarding road bikes.

Wayne Bennett of Don't Push It Mountain Bikes for advice regarding mountain bikes.

Tim Flooks of TF Tuned Shox for advice regarding suspension.

Gerard Brown for his excellent pictures and Guy Andrews for getting together the equipment we needed to show all the aspects of bike maintenance.

Jo Jackson and Keith and Barbara Oldfield for help when the author's computer broke down, twice.

Finally, all the bike companies who lent their equipment for our photoshoots.

Publisher's acknowledgments

This edition additional jacket design by:
Senior DTP Designer Harish Aggarwal, **Jacket Editorial Coordinator** Priyanka Sharma, **Managing Jacket Editor** Saloni Singh

Original edition produced by:
Senior Art Editor Kevin Ryan
Art Editor Michael Duffy,
Managing Editor Adèle Hayward,
Managing Art Editor Karen Self,
Category Publisher Stephanie Jackson, **Art Director** Peter Luff,
DTP Designers Rajen Shah, Adam Shepherd, **Production Controller** Kevin Ward

Design: Janice English, Simon Murrell, Dawn Young

DTP Design: Gemma Casajuana

Photoshoot Art Director: Jo Grey

Picture Research: Carolyn Clerkin

Proofreading: Lynn Bresler, Margaret McCormack

Illustrations: Kevin Jones Associates, Matthew White at Pomegranate Ltd, Tim Loughead at Precision Illustration Ltd.

Additional photography: Jill and Steve Behr at Stockfile

Models: Jay Black, Chris Hopkins, James Millard, Simon Oon, Helen Rosser, Rochele Whyte

Cycling models: Hsu Minh Chung, Jamie Newell, Claire Paginton, Hannah Reynolds, Simon Richardson, Kelli Salone, Ross Tricker, Russell Williams

Accessory, component, and bicycle suppliers:
Ian Young at Moore Large for Schwinn BMX; Caroline Griffiths and Chris Snook at Madison for Electra, Finish Line, Garmin, Park, Profile, Shimano, Ridgeback, Genesis, Cervélo, Commençal; Ross Patterson and Jon Holdcroft at ATB sales for Marin; Collette Clensy at Giant Bikes; Adrian at Pashley bicycles; Evans Cycles in Wandsworth and Milton Keynes; Cedric at Luciano Cycles, Clapham; Sam at Bikepark, Covent Garden; Richard at Apex Cycles, Clapham; Graham at SRAM; Shelley at Continental; Trek UK; Mike Cotty, Cannondale; Richard Pascoe of Ricci—Bike Chain; Fisher Outdoor Leisure; Mark Haylett, Specialized; Gary Anderson, Matt Evans, and Alex Rowling at Chicken Cycle-Kit for Bootleg, Cinelli, Dedacciai, Tifosi, and Nalini; Nick Jones at Corley Cycles UK.

Picture credits

The publisher would like to thank the following for their kind permission to reproduce their photographs:

17: Gerard Brown t; Cervélo b; 18: Aurora Photos / Alamy; 19: Dolan Bikes b; 70—1: Stockfile/ Steve Behr; 164: Fox Racing Shox.

All other images © DK Images.

For further information see www.dkimages.com

PLEASE NOTE

Bicycle maintenance is potentially hazardous. While the information in this book has been prepared with the reader's personal safety in mind, the reader may help reduce the inherent risks involved by following these instructions precisely. The scope of this book allows for some, but not all, the potential hazards and risks to be explained to the reader. Therefore, the reader is advised to adopt a careful and cautious approach when following the instructions, and if in any doubt, to refer to a good bike shop or specialist.